A gift to Fny M. Laughlin

from Ja. ♥ Y0-AGK-895

Life's Interruptions

Life's Interruptions

A Treasury of Hope and Encouragement

Marilyn Whyte / Dorothy Casper

ISBN: 1-55517-046-3

CFI
Cedar Fort Incorporated
1182 North Industrial, Orem, UT 84057 801-226-4004

Lithographed in the United States of America

Dedication

To the eight special families who stories are included in this book; for their willingness to give up some of their privacies and intimacies for the benefit of others.

Table of Contents

Foreword

"The best of a book is not in the thought it contains, but in the thought that it suggests," said Oliver Wendel Holmes. May this work echo the feelings of our hearts as it is written to enlarge the vision, enhance the soul, inspire us to become more worthy sons and daughters of a loving Heavenly Father.

Acknowledgements

Our inexpressible gratitude is extended to those both seen and unseen who have graciously shared their lives, their strength, and their souls that we might more fully understand and grow from life's interruptions. The creative insight and gifted ability of Stuart Hall, as witnessed in the beautiful illustrations, is most appreciated. We are very grateful for our husbands and children, who have given unrelenting support and encouragement. And we humbly thank a wise and loving Heavenly Father, who has allowed each of us to experience difficult and unwanted trials. These "unseen blessings" brought us together and inspired the conception of this rewarding project. What a joyous labor of love!

CHAPTER ONE

Life's Interruptions

Marilyn

Little David had a formidable and fluent vocabulary for a two-year-old, and when his newly adopted father began to teach him of his immortal beginnings, the words of a babe revealed the mysteries of God.

"We used to live up in Heaven with Heavenly Father, David," spoke a loving dad, "even though we can't remember it now."

"But I can remember, Daddy!" came the quick reply.

As Don Duke looked into clear and uplifted innocent eyes, a hush filled his soul and he felt the presence of angels. "Just what is it you can remember, David?"

"Well, Daddy, the most important thing was that Heavenly Father didn't want me to cry when I left."

Nothing like the sweetness and pureness of a little child causes us to ponder our own personal beginnings. Although it is uncertain whether we shed tears upon our departure from premortal realms, it is very certain we have shed many since. Often as we struggle with life's trials and tests, we lose sight of who we really are and that we truly did rejoice at the prospect of proving ourselves in this mortal sphere.

New Dimension of Faith

When some new pain pierces my life
Rebellion begins to cry,
God knew this would come and He approved!
But wait, long ago—so did I.[1]

In the book *All These Things Shall Give Thee Experience*, Elder Neal A. Maxwell offers a new and enlightening perspective on our experiences and trials in this life.

"Life is a school in which we enrolled not only voluntarily but rejoicingly; and if the school's Headmaster employs a curriculum—proven, again and again on other planets, to bring happiness to participants—and if we agree that once we were enrolled there would be no withdrawals, and also to undergo examinations that would truly test our ability

---

[1]"New Dimension of Faith"(Author Unknown)

and perceptivity, what would an experienced Headmaster do, if later on, there were complaints? Especially if, in His seeming absence, many of the school children tore up their guiding notebooks and demanded that He stop the examinations, since these produced some pain. There is . . . no way to 'CLIP' the examinations of the second estate, one learns by taking the full course! 2

But how painful can be the curriculum, whose successful completion offers the highest reward, eternal life. On dark days when the course seems long, we often wonder if we will ever meet the requirements or pass the final exam. On every hand and in every life we see problems and trials, for they are, as is God's love, no respecter of persons. We each entered this earthly school with individual and personal talents and abilities, and we are now in the process of learning to deal with life.

Situations and assignments are varied and even though each enrollee will ultimately have to meet final qualifications, it is hard to understand why nearly everyone in our school seems to have a different course of study. As victims of human nature it seems only natural to try to compare and judge totally different lab experiences in an effort to determine who's getting the highest scores. We can't help but wonder how we are doing. This attempt is always unsuccessful for only He who records the *effort* can see into the heart.

---

2 Neal A. Maxwell, *All These Things Shall Give Thee Experience* (Salt Lake City, UT: Deseret Book, 1979) p. 27.

Meanwhile, our comparison causes us to become discouraged and feel overloaded with endless and seemingly pointless homework.

One of the greatest challenges we face is that life requires us to wait for unanswered questions. We seek to know and understand what is happening to us, as endless interruptions from our point of view, appear to stifle our progress. Expressing mortal frustration, we complain to the 'seemingly absent Headmaster,' "I could learn better—if I knew what it is you are trying to teach me."

The perplexing problems are in reality "masked blessings" that reveal to us ourselves, and ultimately cause every knee to bow beneath the weight of a heavy burden.

The Plea.

But Father, I'm so very tired
Where will it all take me?
I can't remember who I am
Where, or why it all began.

Yesterday seemed so sure, so bright.
My path I knew, now where is light?
Older, yes, and wiser—so
Why can't I sense the way to go?

Somewhere in my inner soul
Must lie the strength. I feel its life,
Feeble, small, though well alive.

Please, help me reach, and bid me rise.[3]

Strength and courage to rise also come as we begin to understand the teachings of Orson F. Whitney and their personal implication in our lives.

"No pain that we suffer, no trial that we experience is wasted. It ministers to our education, to the development of such qualities as patience, faith, fortitude, and humility. All that we suffer and all that we endure, especially when we endure it patiently, builds up our characters, purifies our hearts, expands our souls, and makes us more tender and charitable, more worthy to be called the children of God." [4]

Life often brings a heavy load, and many times we feel inadequate and question our self worth and ability to cope. Great comfort comes in knowing God personally knows us, and our capabilities. The wise Headmaster is schooling us for Eternity. Elder Maxwell teaches that:

"The tests given to us here are given not because God is in doubt as to the outcome, but because we need to grow in order to be able to serve with full effectiveness in the eternity to come." [5]

---

[3] The Plea by Marilyn Whyte, 1989

[4] Spencer W. Kimball, *Tragedy or Destiny* (Salt Lake City, UT: Deseret Book, 1970, p. 26

[5] Neal A. Maxwell, *All These Things Shall Give Thee Experience* (Salt Lake City, UT: Deseret Book, 1979) p. 26.

Years ago I had an experience that changed my perception of this earthly school, forever.

It was months before I could speak of the experience, and I offer it now in humility and testimony that life is eternal, and we are not left in this sphere to find our way alone. The Lord and others under His direction stand by to assist us through an unseen, though very thin, veil.

During my childbearing years, I had become quite accustomed to dealing with physical complications and miscarriage. And here I was again, this time only moments after losing in the doctor's office what would have become my next child. My husband and three small children, also accustomed to emergency runs, sat patiently in the waiting room. As the doctor stepped outside to break the news to Cliff and make arrangements for further treatment at the hospital across town, I sat alone, cold bare feet hanging motionless, holding the bottle I insisted on seeing.

I stared into the solution and counted little fingers and toes. "Who were you meant to be?" My soul yearned to know. "Surely you know and share this moment with me." My hands trembled. I had witnessed this before, but a strange sweeping sickness engulfed me. "Get hold of yourself." I spoke almost audibly and fought to get control of the churning inside. Unassisted and still alone, I made it to the sink and grasped its smooth clean porcelain edges to steady myself. But as I glanced into the mirror, the white, drawn face looking back startled me, and I felt faint.

I experienced no pain or physical trauma, but a heavy feeling of separation and emptiness. "Get hold of yourself. You're all right," I repeatedly told myself and concentrated on moving my fingers as I shakily dressed. In the hall I vaguely heard the nurse asking if they should call for an ambulance to transport me. "No, she'll be fine," the doctor replied, "They can be to the hospital before it gets here." "See, you'll be fine," I told myself again.

I don't remember walking to the four-wheel drive pickup we had brought to combat the snow covered roads, but I was somewhat alarmed to recognize my weakness as Cliff helped me in. Huge white snowflakes filled the sky and blanketed everything in the heavy winter storm. But I felt warm and secure with our three little ones bundled between us.

Then no sooner than we had left the parking lot, I felt a sudden pressure and immediate panic as I realized what was happening. "Hurry!" I said. "I am," Cliff replied as he battled busy traffic in heavy snow with little visibility. "Hurry..." I could only whisper as massive hemorrhage ensued. Fear clutched my heart for only seconds and then disappeared as quickly as it came. I knew I was dying. I was twenty-seven years old, and I wouldn't make it. These were my final moments—my life was over! I looked at my three little ones, and with all the intensity and feeling of my heart, I wanted to hold them one last time. Silently my heart cried, "I love you . . . Good-bye." I was too weak to speak nor could I conceal from them the blood that gurgled and ran over my arms and onto the floor.

And yet a feeling of total peace and comfort came over me. I remember looking towards the window feeling I needed air, and that was the last thing I remembered. As I fell forward, Cliff instinctively reached over and held my head back so I could breathe. He didn't panic or stop the truck because he had seen me faint many times before. Instead he drove (I later learned) like an efficient madman, running red lights, plowing over sidewalks and across corner lots through several feet of heavy snow. Without his cool thinking and a four-wheel drive vehicle, we never would have made it—although technically, I didn't.

When we reached the emergency room, I was classified as "clinically dead." A doctor was not immediately available, but a determined nurse worked frantically and refused to give up. I had no respiration—my pulse was 40 over 0 and all veins had collapsed. Less than one pint of blood was left in my body. After a series of desperate attempts to find a vein in my arms and legs, the nurse was able to begin an IV to pump life-giving glucose water into me. I did not have enough blood to type, so "unmatched" massive transfusions began.

The first thing I was aware of were hollow voices, seemingly shouting orders, with one above the rest—the valiant little nurse who took charge. I found that hearing is the last of the six senses to go, and although the trauma team didn't realize it, I could hear them. I felt separate and aside from the life-saving battle that ensued. I couldn't feel anything, but I could hear the sound of someone slapping my face. Next I was somewhat aware of someone pulling my eyes open and telling me over and over, "You have to try." But I didn't want to. Total peace and serenity surrounded me, and even though I was aware that my children were outside, I did not want to return, and I knew I was not alone. I could feel the presence of someone standing behind my head attending me.

The life-saving blood being pumped into my body was being lost just as quickly, and somehow I knew they were taking me up to surgery. Though I couldn't speak or communicate, a wise, understanding nurse read the frantic look in my eyes and understood. I relaxed as I heard her instruct them to move my children before they wheeled me into the elevator. I did not want them to remember me this way.

The feeling of cold, smooth metal was the next thing I realized as I lay on the operating table. Still present was the warm feeling of someone standing behind my head. In the panic, there had been no time for a priesthood blessing, but now I felt the presence and touch of unseen hands placed upon my head from beyond the veil. A comforting feeling and warm energy flowed down my body and to the ends of my feet as it responded to the power of God.

Again I heard voices—the first, the same nurse who never left my side, inquiring about anesthetic. "She's so far gone she'll never feel a thing," was the reply. I felt my body arch and then heard it slap against the table although there was no pain. A massive dose of PIT in my veins had clamped off the broken artery, and the hemorrhaging ceased.

In the late evening I regained consciousness, and with it came high fevers and sickness as packed blood cells were added to the transfusion tube. Sometime after midnight my body had finally accepted enough blood to survive, and for the first time, I was left alone. I dozed momentarily, but the presence of someone near awakened me. Thinking it was a nurse, I turned over to look, but no one was there. I was all alone in the semi-dark room, and the open door revealed a quiet corridor. I turned back over and closed my eyes and just moments later was reawakened by the presence of someone standing very near my bed. I realized then, beyond any doubt, that I was being attended and watched over by my grandmother. Grandma had taught me to play the piano as a little girl. She was the grandma I had loved and missed since she died when I was nine.

Somehow she knew of my need, and someone had sent her to help me! I felt her sweet radiance and love—and at last feeling completely safe and peaceful, I rested. Several times during the night I reawakened, each time to feel her sweet reassurance that everything would be okay. And I could sleep again. I still remember the wall clock in the dim light saying 5:30 a.m., and as the noise and routine of the hospital quickened, grandma left.

I didn't begin to fully comprehend all that had happened until members of the hospital staff began stopping in to see me later that morning. One doctor from the lab put his head inside my doorway and inquired, "Mrs. Whyte?" As I nodded affirmatively, he stepped in with a beaming smile and said, "So you're the one who died last night! Welcome back!" As everyone kept telling me how lucky I was, I began to understand the miracle that had taken place, and yet, I was intensely bothered by the fact that I didn't want to return. What was wrong with me, and why was I left and not taken? Where did I really belong? I didn't share my feelings with anyone but began to deeply analyze my life.

Until this time, I looked upon life as a system of checks and balances. Judging from a mortal outlook, I thought the Lord would probably just have to "balance the books" on Judgment Day. I had a testimony and had been blessed with many rich spiritual experiences, and I was keenly aware of my faults and weaknesses. I had also contemplated the great final exam and feared I would never pass! My only hope was that the Lord would offset my negative score with "brownie points" I had accumulated from serving Him and trying to do His work. I so wanted to be found worthy! I had accepted every call—regardless of how great or small—and worked diligently to prove myself.

Until I learned that we are not our "performance" or the title we bear (i.e., president, the teacher, or the capable advisor), I even judged my own worthiness by the position to which I was called. I had received leadership positions very young and thought it was necessary to maintain such a record. After carefully observing those who appeared to be very successful in all aspects of life, I determined that if you wanted to play in the big leagues, you had to play big league ball. At the time, it seemed like a reasonable philosophy to me. I considered the Celestial Kingdom to be as "big" as it gets, and I tried desperately to meet the requirements and in so doing did acquire useful knowledge and skills. (But such performance is not mandatory in life's curriculum.)

Little did I know that I didn't need to be concerned with how my "lab assignment" compared with someone else's. The same understanding and lesson in life can be effectively learned in a multitude of assignments and situations. The real proving ground comes with adversity and trial, when the "Headmaster" sees if we will do all things whatsoever He requires, in spite of the circumstances.

When I briefly left and returned to this life that wintry day, I learned that the only thing you take with you is what is in your heart and mind. Nothing more, nothing less. You leave with what you came with— your spirit, and what you have created and gained spiritually, not physically. Rather than the cake you bake or the record of service rendered—what really matters is how that act of service changed your heart. I no longer believe there will be a great and final exam. But we must be very careful not to overlook the "daily quizzes" we experience in the tedious and many times overwhelming trials of life.

When we each have, in our own time and season, completed the course set forth for us here and have met the challenges of life in our own way, we will personally make an accounting for those choices. Then He who looketh upon the heart will invite us to do so with Him, and as we do, we will realize we have already determined our score.

I know, as surely as I know life itself that we are eternal. Even death, the ultimate interruption in our mortal existence, is not the end or the most ominous or difficult step we will be required to take in completing the full course of earthly experience. It is instead a graduation—a great commencement into eternal life.

But in the meantime, the project at hand is living life fully and gleaning from its trials the lessons the Headmaster intended. Nephi of old declared "Men are, that they might have joy," (2 Ne. 2:25), but as we experience the frustrations of daily living, we quickly learn from this "hands on" project that many days are far from joyous. As we become submissive students of the Master, we begin to understand that personal happiness must be developed in spite of the trial.

None of us are likely to leave this school as strangers to sorrow and adversity. An old legend from the Far East tells of a mother who long ago lost a child. Stunned and grief-stricken, in despair she sought out a holy man and pleaded and begged for him to restore the life of her only son. The wise man replied that before he could help her she must first go throughout the land and gather flowers from the doorsteps of only those homes who had never known sorrow. From these flowers she was to prepare a beautiful garland and bring it to him.

The legend tells of her search and how after the passing of time, she returned to the holy man with empty hands. Compassionate eyes met hers as she softly spoke. "I walked many days throughout the land and inquired at every door. But nowhere could I find a home whose family had not known sorrow. I can bring you no flowers, but I can be content with my lot."

As seeds cast to the wind, so are the varied trials and interruptions that come into our lives. President Harold B. Lee taught that, "We . . . have to be tried and tested by poverty, by sickness, by death of loved ones, by temptation, by affluence and riches, by ease and luxury, by false educational ideas, and by the flattery of the world." [6]

We never know what the next "term's" assignment may bring. Perhaps we will be accompanied by the private tutor of pain or guilt. The heavy burden of discouragement may be ours to bear, or a long and painful walk with sorrow may lie ahead. Courses in loneliness, fear, and humility may not only be offered—but may be required.

Major trials come into every life, but on a daily basis we more commonly deal with small nagging worries and tedious concerns. Keeping up with demanding schedules that require all our time and energy can become a great trial in itself. Small interruptions like an incessantly ringing phone, a stalled vehicle, or a child's repeated cry, break our

---

[6] Harold B. Lee, *Stand Ye In Holy Places* (Salt Lake City, UT: Deseret Book, 1979) p. 26.

planned routines and seem to stifle the progress we wanted and needed the day to bring. Even when something major upsets our course, the mundane endless frustrations of daily life continue.

For many, the most substantial problems in life are the accumulation of everyday trials. It has been said that life does not consist mainly or even largely of facts and happenings. It mainly consists of the storm of thoughts that is forever blowing through one's head. Frequently it is not the major trial but the constant breeze blowing through our heads that drives us crazy. Many times this breeze turns into a heavy gale capable of throwing us off course. These daily quizzes produce unwanted pain and we, as Elder Neal A. Maxwell stated, complain to the Headmaster and want the testing stopped!

A more wise and understanding fellow student, Spencer W. Kimball, who through the patient and correct application of the required curriculum became a living prophet, empathized with our feelings and offered prophetic counsel:

"Being human, we would expel from our lives physical pain and mental anguish and assure ourselves of continual ease and comfort, but if we were to close the doors upon sorrow and distress, we might be excluding our greatest friends and benefactors. Suffering can make saints of people as they learn patience, long suffering, and self-mastery." [7]

---

[7] Spencer W. Kimball, *Tragedy Or Destiny* (Salt Lake City, UT: Deseret Book, 1977), p. 4.

The greatest challenge in life and the desired outcome of our schooling is to know God and become like Him. Many times "unwanted" tutoring from the Lord reveals to each of us a new world—for it opens the door within. And what lies within? We have been taught that we, as intelligent beings, in the image of God, possess in embryo every organ, attribute, sense, sympathy, and affection that is possessed by God Himself. Graduating from this school with honors requires sanctification and the development of these qualities.

Knowing that all of us fear the intense heat of the refiner's fire, a loving Headmaster promises us: "The flame shall not hurt thee; I only design Thy dross to consume and thy gold to refine." [8] And thus through the lessons of life, He burns from our souls pride and envy, anger and strife. Our hearts are cleansed of the dross (the unwanted and useless), and fear is expelled by faith. Bitterness and contention are replaced with love and peace, and we learn to be more like Him. Orson F. Whitney taught, "It is through sorrow and suffering, toil and tribulation, that we gain the education that we came here to acquire and which will make us more like our Father and Mother in heaven."[9]

Life becomes more meaningful when, in our course of study, we acquire more than the temporary awards and honors of the world. As we come to

---

[8] "How Firm A Foundation," *Hymns*, 1985, no. 85.
[9] Spencer W. Kimball. *Tragedy Or Destiny* (Salt Lake City, UT: Deseret Book, 1977), p. 4.

understand what we were sent here to accomplish and
what really matters in the final evaluation, daily living
takes on a new level and our eternal vision becomes
clear.

Insights

I see a Vision
    my sons tall and straight
    with eyes seeing in the sun
    a new day, a brighter tomorrow.
I see my life's desire
    once a dream, now becoming a reality.

I have lived, striving for a breaking
    from the past, and bonding with the
    future a new perspective—
        a clearer outlook, molding former
        lessons
        into foundations of finer living.

I see my mistakes
    and desire them not repeated.
I see my wisdom wrought from painful
    experience
    and pray it be the foothold from
    which my children spring.

I see a finer view
    the blessings of a fuller life,
    a purer existence—

For I have lived for the Vision.[10]

This is a book of hope, written to help us retain our vision as we are required to take difficult steps and endure clouded days of sorrow and despair. It is an honest and open look at the varied interruptions of life and the intense emotions they evoke. The people and the situations in the following stories are real and the names have *not* been changed.

When pain pierces our hearts, it is natural to turn to those who have also suffered and understand. Each of the friends you are about to meet have also felt the flame of the refiner's fire and have stood faithfully on the proving ground of adversity. Their insight offers hope, inspiration, and hard-won wisdom.

Although the style, design, and pattern of each individual's life varies (as the Lord intended it would), interwoven into the fabric of life are common threads of faith, determination, and simplicity. Their sincere, although diversified, expressions of encouragement and love show forth the Hand of God. Life, as seen through their eyes, becomes more than a series of interruptions and trials, being instead a necessary and continual process of eternal growth.

---

10 Marilyn Whyte, 1989.

CHAPTER TWO

You Just Go On

Zoanne

*"She gently offers her hand in understanding,
and we are lifted to higher ground."*

"When you can't stand it any longer, go into your
bedroom and scream," counselled the humorous note
attached to a bright and cheery bouquet of flowers.
Gloom and frustration were dispelled, and gratefully
received was this token of love, delivered by a friend
who knew and understood. Once again, Zoanne had
quietly recognized a need, unseen by others, and
reached out to lift and encourage. She knew and
understood sorrow, despair, and discouragement.
Though beautiful the flowers were, the most lasting
and priceless gift was the spirit and strength of the
giver.

Life provides that every soul cries for help in the extremity of suffering. Why is this happening? What is life for? What does God want me to do with this? We all know feelings of being at our rope's end and that we just can't take any more. We cry for release that often doesn't come. Grateful are we for those who reach to us and tell us we can.

"Difficulties are the things that show what men are" (Epectitus). Elder Hugh B. Brown taught that, "If we banish hardship, we banish hardihood. . . . One man's disillusion may be another's inspiration. The same exposure to pain, misery, and sorrow that coarsens the mind of one may give another a power of compassionate understanding and humility without which, mere achievement remains primitive." [1]

Life and its difficulties have revealed Zoanne Murdock to be a beloved and elect lady of the Lord. An "elect lady" is one chosen to do a certain work, and Zoanne, quietly and faithfully, labors daily in the Lord's service. We often look to the past or to faraway places for great examples of courageous and valiant women. Perhaps we should avert our vision to the present, within our own realm, to learn from the majesty and inner might of those who live next door. We admire courageous souls whose shoes we think we could never fill and, at the same time, contemplate our own inadequacies. Joseph F. Smith once said of Eliza R. Snow, "She walked not in borrowed light of others,

---

[1] "Salvation Is My Goal," *New Era*, (December, 1974): p. 7.

but faced the morning light unafraid and invincible." [2] And yet, at one time Eliza was "just a friend next door."

Today, as in the past, a loving Father places His strongest children "just next door" to help light the way for us. As with most great women, Zoanne is so given in natural kindness and consideration that she seems unaware of the power and example she possesses.

Experience and sorrow have developed within her a deep sense of understanding. Her life—lived calmly and serenely—stands as a tower of strength to those around her. These attributes, acclaimed by others, to Zoanne are just a part of life as she has maintained a steady course in the face of adversity.

"I really don't like to tell people what has happened to me," Zoanne stated. "I don't want them to think, 'You poor person' or feel sorry for me. I want them to like me for who I am. That's what everyone needs regardless of their situation. But there are so many alone, we need to reach out to them." And so she reaches to share that we may have strength to abide the day.

"I remember about seven years ago, sitting in family home evening with Denis and our seven children on a Monday night. I looked up and caught Denis's eye from across the room and without a word, I knew he was feeling exactly as I did, as peace and contentment surrounded us. It was just like being in heaven. Nothing could have been more special than the

---

[2] Carol Lynn Pearson, *Daughters of Light* (Salt Lake City, UT: Publisher's Press, 1973) p. 10.

love and unity we shared as a family. I shall never forget that moment."

Short months later, tragic events would change their lives forever. But Zoanne's story really begins long before that special Monday night.

"Line upon Line"

We enter this life with intelligence, and life adds to it knowledge and experience. Obedience brings wisdom, followed by the crowning achievement of understanding. All of God's children learn line upon line and step by step. The Lord had prepared Zoanne for the overwhelming challenges that lay ahead. Many times as difficulties came, she would find reliance on the strength she had developed in youth.

Zoanne enjoyed a normal and happy childhood in the small rural community of Thomas, Idaho. Being the oldest child, her father treated her like a princess, and she realized very young that she couldn't take advantage of him—not because she couldn't get away with it, but because he would do anything in his power for his little angel. Numerous were childhood friends, but nearest and dearest was her mother. School came easy to this slight, but energetic, little girl and although she always did well, she never seemed to dwell on her own abilities. As a senior, she was pleased and "amazed" to be among the top ten in her graduating class.

In retrospect, Zoanne realized that we often learn more from what we lack than from what we possess. As with most of their neighbors, the young family struggled financially during their early years. Zoanne recalls feeling fortunate and blessed to have two pairs of shoes and two dresses. Her best friend and many other girls had only one of each to be worn for both school and church. In the third grade, Zoanne needed glasses that the family simply couldn't afford. Loving parents had started a savings account for Zoanne and her younger brother from saved pennies, dimes, and nickels. The only option was to draw out the accumulated $49.00 to pay for the glasses and buy lunch tickets for the two little ones next month at school.

She recalled, "I never felt poor. In the sixth grade, full skirts with flounce slips were the fad. I had picked out a $3.00 dress for school. It was nice, but it didn't have a big full slip. One day some of the girls made fun of me. I felt bad, but at the same time, I knew it was all my folks could afford. I thought, 'So what!' But deep inside it really hurt, although I never let it show. In high school, Mother taught me to sew, and I always felt confident and that what I had was okay. I had developed self-reliance, for I knew I could handle and grow from my experiences. I think those conditions really strengthened me. Having everything you want is a real disadvantage. Now my wants don't outdo my needs.

"You never realize the examples your parents have been to you until you are grown. We had family prayer every morning, and if Dad was late from work in the evening, Mom always waited to eat with him.

Every morning I saw Dad kiss her good-bye, and to this day she still sits by him in the car. I have received great strength from the testimony of a righteous life I received as a child at home."

When she met her sweetheart the summer after her first year at college, Zoanne had a strong foundation for the kind of home and family she desired. She had known Denis Murdock's fine parents and family for years and had even gone to school with his younger brother. The two families had summer cabins near each other at Island Park, but Denis was four and a half years older, and somehow they had never met. He had been home from his mission for two and a half years when he and Zoanne met at a church party and became good friends. They dated the whole summer, and love gradually blossomed and grew, based on a strong and enduring friendship and mutual goals and aspirations. The following November they were engaged and then married in the Idaho Falls Temple on January 29, 1965. Zoanne was twenty. Two strong families had united for the beginning of an eternal posterity that would bless and inspire many. Thus had Zoanne's second great strength entered her life: marrying a good man with a fine background. Together they would build a home based on the teachings of their parents. As a young and willing new mother in a college ward, Zoanne was impressed with a little handout, written by an unknown author, brought her by visiting teachers. She put it on the fridge and daily read the words that became deeply imprinted in her heart.

Your task, to build a better world, God Said;
I answered, How?
This world is such a large vast place,
So complicated now,
And I so small and useless am,
There's nothing I can do.

But God in all his wisdom said,
Just build a better you.

Great and far-reaching becomes the influence of
a woman who chooses to live her life well. And now,
almost two decades later, Denis and Zoanne enjoyed
the fruits of their labor as they sat with their children
in family home evening. Both felt the bond of their
eternal unit, now strong and united because they had
faced and overcome many trials raising this fine
family of three girls and four boys.

"Our Problems Were Definitely a Blessing"

"All of life's experiences bring you something.
Sometimes our adversities are really our blessings,"
states Zoanne. During the early years of our marriage,
Denis spent most of his time working on the farm
trying to make a living. This meant that he had to
spend too much time away from the children. On
Sundays he was in meetings all day with church
assignments, and the rest of the week he was out on
the farm. At one time he had not seen the kids for two

full weeks. Early one Sunday morning, our oldest daughter, Sandy, a teenager, stopped on her way down the hall and leaned on the bathroom door and watched Denis shave. She said, "Oh, so you're the man that lives here that I never see. It's you, my missing dad." She and Denis were extremely close and the truth of her statement upset Denis so badly that he resolved to change the priorities in our lives.

We had gotten so big in the farming business, and some setbacks forced us to cut back the operation. The next summer Denis didn't plant potatoes but only raised grain, and he bought the family a boat.

We water skied together as a family several times a week all summer, and we had a ball. Our problems were definitely a blessing, although at the time Denis felt like he had failed monetarily. I tried to assure him that though he may have had some failure farming, he was successful in the things that really matter most for eternity—his family. A man's occupation is his life and a setback in business is a trauma. Men frequently bear feelings of failure that they really don't need to. When it's all said and done, you can't take anything with you but your family. But it is sometimes hard to keep that perspective in this life.

Life offers many experiences, but the real teacher is adversity.

Seven years earlier, the Murdock's oldest son Mark, who was six, and his four-year-old brother, Alan were playing with matches in a shed behind the house. As they were burning holes in their shirts with candles, Mark's shirt suddenly ignited and engulfed him in flames. Fortunately, little Alan was able to put out the fire and save his brother's life. Mark's coat protected his arms but he suffered third-degree burns all over his stomach, chest, and neck. His face, nose and ear lobes were also seriously burned. For the next two weeks, he lay in a serious condition in a croup tent at a local hospital. But after a priesthood blessing, Zoanne felt comforted and assured that she wouldn't lose her son at that time. It was as though someone said, "He will be fine, but he has much to go through yet.".

When he became stable enough to be taken to a burn specialist in Salt Lake, redness from the burns could no longer be seen above his chin. As the doctor read the report, he immediately recognized the miracle. The remaining burns were so extensive, the Murdocks were advised that several operations would be required to complete the grafting. A long and painful week of debriding the burns at the Primary Children's Hospital required the suffering of both parents and child. After the graft, Mark was confined to an upper-body cast until Christmas.

As carollers visited his ward to sing, they would stand tearfully at his door as he sang for them. "Give, said the little stream's" pure and sweet tones touched their hearts, as this little boy, lying completely still, returned their love. Patiently he waited as painfully stripped thighs and hips began to heal, eventually scarred as deeply as his neck and chest.

The day to remove the bandages came just before Christmas, but the doctors advised there was no possibility of Mark's going home for the holiday. Miraculously only one small spot had not taken, and on December 21, Mark went home for Christmas. The little family's united prayers and faith had been answered. But new trials awaited Mark.

When he returned to school, older kids poked fun, and it upset him when adults stared and asked, "What happened to you?" Not wanting to tell them, he gradually became a loner and always wore a turtle neck sweater to cover his scars. A special teacher in the sixth grade resolved to help Mark become more outgoing with the boys. Suddenly there were friends on every side, and boys were constantly visiting the Murdock home.

The summer after the seventh grade, Mark attended a scout leadership camp at Lemhi. He was scheduled to come home the Friday before Father's Day, but the preceding Sunday Denis had the strongest desire to visit his son. Zoanne reminded him that they didn't want parents at camp, but Denis said he was going anyway. He was exhausted from spring work, so Zoanne offered to drive and Denis, with four-year-old Michael on his lap, slept most of the way. An hour and a half later they pulled into camp, just in time to see Mark come running down the hill with some new friends. Out of breath, he inquired why they were there, and they replied they came just to see him. Zoanne said he talked all of two minutes and was gone. "That's all we saw of him. We turned around and

came home and wondered why we had made the trip."
Mark returned home full of excitement and energy and
enjoyed Father's Day with his family.

"It was Unbelievable. . . ."

The following Tuesday, June 21, 1983, began as
typical summer day at the Murdock home. It dawned a
rainy morning, and Zoanne sent Mark, 13, and Alan,
12, to clean the shop while she cared for the little ones.
They returned for lunch, and then Zoanne prepared for
the missionaries who were coming to teach a family
that worked for Denis. As they were teaching, she lay
down with two-year-old Merilee for a nap so she
wouldn't disturb them.

Around 6 p.m. Mark needed to be delivered to the
church for a scout meeting, and as usual most of the
children wanted to go along for the ride. They stopped
at a nearby busy intersection and waited for traffic to
clear, when the driver's view was tragically blinded by
the sun's intense brilliant glare. As the family pulled
onto the roadway they were struck by an oncoming
potato truck. Mark, four-year-old Michael, and tiny
Merilee were killed instantly.

Having no inclination that anything was going
to happen, Zoanne was shocked when a kind neighbor
knocked at her door. It was unbelievable! Her brother
had gone in search of Denis, who met Zoanne at the
hospital. Later, they went to the mortuary where they
were allowed to see two of the children. Little Michael
had suffered such severe head injuries that they were

unable to view his body. The couple received great comfort that although Merilee was thrown the farthest from the car, she looked as if she had gone to sleep without any trauma. The spirit of the Lord attended, and peace filled the air. Young Mark, lying on the table with a light surrounding him, seemed to be a full-grown man.

Shock and grief paralyzed the community as everyone mourned the enormous loss as the three children were buried side by side. Hands reached and hearts yearned to know how to help or offer comfort. "How can you handle it?" sorrowed friends. Souls stretched to understand. "You can't understand; don't try to understand," Zoanne later reflected. "Just be here, just listen. Just speak to me and recognize I'm here."

"About a month before the kids died, I looked into Michael's room and thought, 'What would I ever do without him?' The pain was so great I couldn't stand it, and I blocked it from my mind. How could I ever bear it?

"When someone has those kinds of thoughts, they turn them off because the pain is unbearable to the conscious mind. I used to look at others and wonder how they could stand it. When we have never experienced such grief, we can turn the pain off or shut it out. But when it really happens, there is no turning it off. It is always there day and night. People fear how they would handle the same situation and I think that's probably why they say to me. 'You're doing so well.' It's hard to even contemplate losing someone you love, let alone facing the reality. You don't know how you would handle it; you simply don't know. When people back off, it isn't that they don't care. They don't understand or know what to do.

"I don't like people to look at me and say, 'You handle things so well.' I think, 'Huh?' I don't do any better than the next person. I just do what I have to do, and others do what they have to do. It bothers me when I hear that, even if I'm feeling well enough to handle that day, I'm not doing any better than others do. You can't judge someone without knowing his limits, and only our Father knows those. The Lord allows these things to happen; He doesn't cause them. We cannot see His overall plan. In this life we do not see beyond our own little needs. The Lord knows all things."

Zoanne immediately felt the presence of the Holy Ghost after the children's deaths. Mark's presence stayed for nearly a month until Denis performed his temple work, as if he were anxiously awaiting it, and then his presence left. "No one came and removed my children's possessions. That was my privilege. I still have things I'm not ready to part with, but someday I will," stated Zoanne.

"Over the years, I've learned not to cry in public. People feel sorry that they said something to make you feel bad, and the next time they are hesitant to talk. We've changed holiday traditions and now take trips or go skiing instead. We have tried to find new ways to share those days together, and yet handle our loss. Anniversaries and birthdays are especially hard, but we've learned to live one day at a time."

"Children with Burdens to Bear"

The surviving children not only had to face the loss but also the resultant "labelling" from society. Everywhere they went people watched from the corner of curious eyes to see how they would react or handle the situation if anyone mentioned "the family." I just wanted to be liked for me and not have everyone turn their heads when I walk into class and wonder what I am thinking," was the sorrowful plea so often heard in the Murdock home.

Alan carries within him the painful trauma of the tragedy. He remained conscious and watched in what seemed to be slow motion the entire scene as the two little ones were thrown out. When he saw the truck coming, he heard a voice tell Merilee and Michael to "Lay down and go to sleep." He didn't know until later of Mark's death. He thought Mark was asleep in the back of the car, and overnight in the hospital he assumed his brother was in the room next to him. Many sleepless nights remain a painful part of Alan's life. Once able to save and protect his brother's life, this young lad of twelve was now required to witness his departure. Alan carries a spiritual knowledge deep within that few in this life will ever experience. "As bad as I want to help my children," said Zoanne, "there is nothing I can really do. They have to find a way to handle the things they face in their own way. My heart cries for them."

Denis and Zoanne's family and extended family and friends began to know first hand the stages of grief. Any major loss in our lives is accompanied by the grief process which generates a maximum of intensified feelings. These intensified emotions produce a yo-yo effect in daily living.

"It is unfair and unrealistic to compare grief. Everyone has a different rate of recovery, and life's problems fall into different categories," commented Zoanne. "The solutions are always different because each person has agency in action. But it really helps if you have a little reserve; if you already know the Lord a little bit, and you have had some experiences in life that let you know you can make it. As we struggle in our pain, we must hold fast to our faith in the Lord."

From Sorrow to Solace

Grief involves several stages, and there is no correct order or time frame for each. Some are very long and others very short. These stages can overlap and frequently reoccur long after you think you have worked through those feelings. The grief process cannot be demanded or controlled. As Zoanne said, "You can't just say, 'All right, I'm going to quit grieving now, and I'm going to get better.' It takes a lot of time, and we have to learn to just hang on one day at a time."

The more the trauma or loss affects our daily lives, the longer it takes to work through it. A newspaper survey asked people how long they thought

the normal mourning time was. The average answer
was 48 hours to two weeks. But when 1,200 mourners
were asked how long it took them to work through their
sorrow, the average answer was 18 months to two
years. The time varies, and even after long periods of
time, things trigger setbacks and feelings skyrocket.
Those associated with Sudden Infant Death Syndrome
consider three years an average mourning time.
Compassionate friends and organizations for those
who have lost children say it takes about five years.

Understanding the emotions of grief helps us to
work through them. And it is vital that we do, for grief
not resolved lasts a lifetime.

(The reader will note many of these emotions
reappear in following chapters though circumstance
and problems vary.)

Shock and Denial

In the first stage of grief the soul cries out, "No,
this can't be happening to me," or "There must be a
mistake. It can't be true!" As Zoanne said, "It was just
unbelievable." Numbness fills the mind and body. It is
like viewing in third person what really happened.
You feel you're not really there. It has been said that
denial is nature's sedative for things we can't stand to
bear.

"You always have the Holy Ghost comforting you
at first. It's amazing what you're able to do the first
two months, but when it wears off, you begin to spiral

downward and you and your brain seem to be unable to function together."

Anger

After the numbness wears off, and the "not me" stage has passed, and the next thoughts may be "why me? What have I done to deserve this?" We project our pain in anger. We may search for a place to lay our blame, whether at God for allowing such a thing to happen or lay it at our own feet. "If only I hadn't done this or that." We may blame the one who caused the accident or even turn our pain on our own mate causing tremendous marital strife. Studies show that a large number of couples who have lost a child, divorce.

I can see how that happens. Couples depend on each other so much emotionally, and a spouse simply can't take away the pain as you always sort of expect them to.. Sometimes I would get frustrated and think, "Why can't you make this better? "

"Denis and I learned after the children's accident that even though we were partners, we couldn't really help each other when we were grieving so deeply ourselves. You can't expect that comfort to come from another. You can be supportive, but you have to find your own way out of depression. You can't depend on the other one to do that for you because they are already handling all they can. Just going through it together is help and support, but I could never take his load and he could never take mine."

As Zoanne experienced this stage of grief, she felt anger towards the Lord for allowing the accident to happen. She said, "I was YW president at the time, and I felt that we were doing everything that we could to raise those kids. We had even had the missionaries teaching in our home that very day. I was so bitter and angry that I couldn't even make myself go to the temple. I told my bishop my feelings, and he knew that I needed time and that someday I would overcome those feelings. And I did, although it took several months before I went back to renew my recommend. As I sat in his office, I *knew* my children were there. That's one of the few times I literally felt their presence. They were there because they knew their mother had resolved the bitterness and was ready to get on with life."

Guilt

The next step many experience is feeling guilty for their feelings, and depression follows.

When the rage and anger has finally exhausted itself, despair often takes over. This is the time of deepest sorrow. Realization of the finality of what has happened hits and stays constantly up front in our thoughts. The sufferer can think of nothing else and life becomes disorganized. It is simply hard to function under the black cloud of depression that follows one around night and day. Eventually the sun comes through, and then it is suddenly gone again. You may even find you have gone backwards into one of the other stages. Just when you thought you had conquered anger, you may awake one morning full of resentment.

There is a searching and yearning for familiar sights and sounds or images while longing to have the person back. It is during this time that we ask questions and seek to know answers. "What do I do now?" We turn to those around us, and this is the time when support is needed most.

At this time the Holy Ghost has left us. "If He didn't leave us, we wouldn't grow and learn on our own. We each must face our own Gethsemane."

Physical activity and someone to talk to are almost essential in the healing process. Zoanne found the blessings and benefits of walking each day with a close friend. Many have found talking one of the greatest cures for grief. It allows the sufferer to talk it out, deal with it, and then put it away. But the appropriate time for talking varies with the individual as we each handle life's pain differently. Time itself adds to the healing process.

The final stage of grief is acceptance. We get to the point that we have dealt with the trauma so long and have given it all the strength and energy we can possibly give. Only then are we ready to move forward in our lives and become productive.

"Every person bears his own grief in his own personal trial. We can be there for each other even as mates, but we can't take away another's pain. We look upon men as the protectors in life and have an emotional dependency on them. But how can anyone protect us from death and pain?"

Denis' life changed after the children's deaths, and he handled his grief differently than Zoanne. Added to his sorrow were financial problems nearly everyone in the little agricultural community understood firsthand. He found it difficult to openly deal with his grief. Believing the children were in such a better place, he felt he should be strong and not grieve for them. Zoanne saw Denis become depressed from deeply internalized sorrow, although she supposed he never realized what was wrong. Being able to go into the bedroom and cry helped her to go on the next day. But Denis felt that if he let down and revealed his weakness, he would show that he didn't think the Lord knew what was best.

The Murdock family now consisted of mother and father, seventeen-year-old Sandy, fifteen-year-old Kerrie, twelve-year-old Alan, and eight-year-old Philip.

"We had thought we had all our family but decided to leave it in the Lord's hands, and the next June little Mathew was born. I think the Lord sent him not only to help our family then, but also to help me for what lay ahead."

Another special blessing that strengthened the family was a visit from Elder L. Tom Perry, who was in the area for a wedding. He visited in the Murdock home and gave priesthood blessings of peace and comfort.

Zoanne's trials were not over; she would next be called upon to part with her companion.

Denis became very close to the Lord after the children's accident. He laboriously studied the scriptures and bore his testimony at every opportunity. To know the Savior personally became his ultimate goal in life.

Zoanne recalled, "He used to go into the den and study the scriptures until early in the morning. It frequently upset me as I felt very neglected," said Zoanne. "Knowing the Lord and becoming close to Him seemed to be his whole ambition in life, with everything else a mere sideline. If Denis did not see the Savior personally, he knew of His presence. One night he came out of the den, and when I awoke, he was literally shining. He couldn't talk to me about it at that time. I was still dealing with recurring anger, and I wasn't ready to make the sacrifice to get that close to the Lord."

In April of 1986, just three years after the children's passing, Denis and a close friend prepared to fly to Salt Lake to pick up a friend Denis had taught in the mission field in Australia. He was attending general conference, and they were going to bring him to Idaho for a visit.

"Denis invited me to go, and I wanted to because I love to fly, but my bathroom wasn't cleaned and I didn't want our guest to see it dirty. So I said, "No, you go, and I'll have lunch ready when you get back." The pair had just left Blackfoot and travelled ten miles south when the plane came apart mid-air, and the wing and tail section fell off; both men died in the crash.

Once again there was no inclination that this would happen, and it came as another enormous shock.

When I learned of Denis' death, my first thought was, "I'm glad I didn't go because my children will need me." And they do. I know that's why I'm still here. My children just couldn't handle losing both parents after what they had been through. But I would have gladly been dead that night. So many had come to offer love and support that it was late into the night before I even had a chance to go into the bathroom. I felt like I was having a heart attack and called for my mother in the other room. The chest pains were terrible, and I was in cold sweats and throwing up. 'Mom, what in the world will my children do if something happens to me now?' Again the Holy Ghost attended me. You couldn't handle a major problem like that without the immediate attendance of the Spirit."

In numbness and shock, the family buried Denis on April 14, 1986, next to his children. They then tried to face what life had given them. "I am trying to teach my children," stated Zoanne, "no matter what happens, you just go ahead." And we did.

"Our oldest daughter Sandy was engaged to be wed in just three weeks. The invitations were already addressed, and we had made her wedding gown and all the preparations were complete. She graduated from Ricks three days after the funeral, and three weeks later we went to the temple and she was married. It was quite an adjustment to say the least, but the Lord seemed to stand right at our side. The end of May our second daughter, Kerrie, graduated from high school. It's truly amazing what you're able to do the first two months, but when the numbness wears off, once again you seem to spiral downward, and it becomes hard to function.

"One thing people need to know is that when you hit a low with a serious problem, you're not going to be exempt from other problems. Minor things like burning dinner or a cut knee almost send you into a tail spin because you don't know how to deal with them. And larger problems really throw you into a loop. We are not exempt from the rest of life because we are dealing with a major trial. Sometimes it is very overwhelming, but we need to realize that the Lord is not punishing us. It is just a part of life. You handled things before, and somehow you will be able to handle things again. Just do the best you can right now."

Once again the multiple stages of grief returned. Zoanne felt that the deep sorrow stage seems most painful. "The hardest thing I have to do is go to church on Sunday and look around and see families together. In sorrow your soul cries, "Why me? Everyone seems to be blessed. How come it had to be me? Everyone who has dealt with *any* major sorrow understands those feelings."

Again Zoanne felt the anger return into her life. This time, instead of directing it toward the Lord for not preventing the tragedy, she found she felt anger towards Denis for leaving her. Smiling through tears of frustration in her own good-humored manner, she said, "When I get over there I'm going to have a word with him. It isn't fun trying to raise a family by yourself. I know he probably doesn't have any problems over there. My first question will be, 'And what have you been doing?' Then a more somber spirit settled upon her countenance and she added, "I know Denis didn't have a choice, but I don't think too many people are allowed to stay here after getting so close to the Lord and the other side. . . . I'm not saying his accident was meant to be, and it really doesn't matter anyway. You learn to go around it and live with it and carry on. You can't live the rest of your life in sorrow. Life is for the living and it is to be lived daily. We're not to end it or desire to leave early. We're here to make the most of what we've got. You have to develop skills to work around the sorrow and learn to find other ways to make life happy."

After Denis' death, Zoanne chose to carry on the family farm operation. She is the first to admit that women do not have the same emotional or physical makeup as men to step in and take over a business. But she does have the determination and know-how with the help and support of her father-in-law and brother.

"People wonder why on earth I do it. The answer is simple. I do it for my children. It provides for them and gives them the opportunity to appreciate hard work, and it offers a close association with other fine men." I hate the weight of debt, and the responsibility of taking charge of my life, but I can't leave it until I have raised my sons."

Zoanne is determined to succeed and meet the task at hand, whether gripping the wheel of the farm pickup or soothing a child's needs or extending herself in service of others.

"I am strong some days and very weak on others, and sometimes I'm hard on myself. You must know yourself and recognize your plusses and minuses. I don't like my minuses, but I can accept myself for what I am," she noted.

Although she doesn't want to be known for what has happened to her, she is truly who she is today because of the experiences in her life, and said, "I've learned we can choose how we accept what happens to us. We can either become bitter, or we can find things outside the problem to make us happy.

"Perhaps the greatest lesson I have learned is patience and the realization that this thing and its loneliness will not be resolved easily or swiftly. My greatest challenge is raising a family alone, and my greatest pain is seeing my children suffer; such sorrow is only understood by those who share it. My greatest need and desire is to have other men take a more active interest in my sons.

"My counsel is to enjoy every day with your loved ones. Find something good each day while you have them. We never know what may lie ahead, for none of us are immune to the trials and interruptions in life.

"Knowing I am a literal daughter of Heavenly Father is my greatest strength. It takes a lifelong process to grasp and know and truly understand that concept. We are survivors here, and when we stand before the Lord someday, He will be able to say, 'Well done my child, enter into my presence."

CHAPTER THREE

A New Melody

Natalie

*"A new melody, a richer and purer sound;
beautifully played on a more finely tuned instrument."*

It was Friday, the 13th day of October, 1978.
Welland Hansen turned to a Spanish fellow working in
the potato cellar and said, "You know, here in America
we look upon Friday the 13th as an unlucky day!" They
both smiled and shrugged, weary from a long harvest
season that had already seemed unlucky. Equipment
and weather problems had taken the annual task into
the fall, and everyone was tired.

Welland had farmed in the Rockford area many
years and was now in partnership with his married
son, Zane. Also working for the first time were the two

youngest Hansen girls, Michelle and Natalie. They had asked to work year after year, and Welland always refused their desire, feeling it was too dangerous. But this fall he had consented to let them work, now that Natalie was fourteen and Michelle, thirteen.

The girls had worked day after day for nearly three weeks cleaning clods and vines from a picking table as the potatoes were unloaded from large trucks into the cellar. Late in the afternoon Natalie was tired and wanted to see how many potatoes were left to unload. She reached with her left arm to lift up the rubber flap at the end of the truck bed. But as she did, her right hand dropped, and the light-weight jersey glove protecting it was caught by rollers that drove the unloading belt. Instantly, her hand and forearm were pulled into an unmerciful grinding hold.

Tragically, the manufacturer had not welded on a required safety shield to prevent such an accident. The two large rollers ran off an electric motor and were geared down to have tremendous power and pull. Installed without guards and unseen from above, they were able to snag the edge of Natalie's glove and pull her hand into their horrible grip.

As she screamed, one of the boys ran to turn off the power to prevent the rollers from pulling her to her death. But Natalie was trapped up to her forearm in the machinery.

Engulfed in excruciating pain, she could neither sit nor stand. Alert and aware as her father and others worked desperately to free her, Natalie hung in physical agony. "Please help me, Dad," she cried over and over as her body writhed with pain.

Someone went for Zane who was on a tractor as an anguished father immediately reacted to free his suffering daughter. Frantic thoughts raced through his mind:

"I had a cutting torch nearby, but I knew I would burn her if I tried to cut bearings off the end of the shaft that held the roller. So the first thing I did was cut the rubber belt in the twenty-foot bulk bed, and we pulled it out. That gave us a little more slack, but there was still no way to free her hand. It was a terrible experience as she was in intense pain the entire time. Piece by piece, I had to take it apart as Natalie screamed and cried and begged for me to help her. With a shaking hand holding an allen wrench, I desperately worked on the rusted ends to remove the bearings. Finally, after thirty minutes that seemed like an eternity, we freed her."

Natalie, assisted by her father, somehow walked to the pickup as Zane carefully held her still gloved, but irreparably damaged, right hand. Emergency care was ably given at the Blackfoot Medical Clinic some ten miles away. But as the doctor quickly assessed the damage, he immediately ordered an air ambulance to the University Medical Center in Salt Lake City. The crushing of the rollers had severed all the blood vessels and mangled the bones so badly that her hand was extended six inches beyond its normal length and appeared as if it had been through a grinder.

Welland was overcome with shock and grief at his daughter's suffering, and though emotionally unable to assist, he stood close by as the doctor and the hospital administrator laid hands upon Natalie's head and gave her a priesthood blessing. Forty-five minutes later, with hand packed in ice and attended by three trauma nurses, Natalie was airborne and on her way to Salt Lake.

That afternoon Bobbie Lou, Natalie's mother, had gone with a friend to run errands in a nearby town, and they returned home later than they had planned. Days later, Bobbie Lou realized that the Lord had kept her away from the terrible tragedy taking place at home. Not witnessing the trauma and experiencing resulting emotional drain helped her remain strong through the trials immediately ahead. "I felt whatever was going to be was how the Lord wanted it, and I could accept it."

The air ambulance had already landed in Salt Lake when Welland reached Bobbie Lou. They prayed in the car and anxiously began the 200-mile drive to Salt Lake. By the time they reached the Medical Center, Natalie had already undergone a three-hour operation. It was the first of seven that would follow in the next five weeks.

Saturday was a day of waiting and praying that warmth would return to the lower arm and hand indicating restored circulation. The night before, skilled surgeons worked feverishly to repair delicate nerve endings and blood vessels, and pins were installed to hold shattered bones in place. The threat of gangrene and the possibility of losing the entire arm allowed the doctors to wait only a maximum of 36 hours for the tissue to show signs of repair. If not, immediate action would be required, or Natalie could lose her life.

Being heavily sedated and in shock, reality was a blur to this fourteen-year-old child. Her body was completely packed in ice to combat high fever and infection. Regular shots for pain and antibiotics had to be changed frequently as their effectiveness wore off quickly.

Natalie recalled, "When they told me what was happening, I was in a state of numbness and disbelief. How long will it take?" I asked. "I've got to be home tomorrow to play the piano in Jr. Sunday School." She was a talented organist, and she loved her calling. "I promised I wouldn't miss! I've got to let them know!" Her inner spirit rang true and clear amid her suffering, but the melody of Natalie's life would be changed forever.

The heartbreaking news came Sunday morning that the hand must be amputated. Bobbie Lou had many relatives in the Salt Lake Valley, and they gathered in a room at the hospital for a special family prayer. As the Thomas 3rd Ward and many from the community at home fasted for her, Natalie received another priesthood blessing. The psychiatric counselor on the children's floor stayed close to the three as the surgery hour approached. Before scheduled amputee patients undergo surgery, they are heavily sedated and only moments away from being wheeled from their room they are told of the procedure. This helps to keep anxiety and fear controllable and is in the patient's best interest medically.

The counselor first gently spoke of family who we love and sometimes lose. Then she told Natalie that her arms and legs are a part of her body's personal family.

"You are going to lose part of your arm. It will be like losing a part of your family. You will think of your poor little hand like you might think of a poor little sister. You will miss it." It isn't something to try to put behind or never think about. It will be a part of you that you can't change, an interruption in your life that you will have to work around.

Signing the release forms and then seeing their daughter wheeled away caused Welland and Bobbie Lou extreme emotional and spiritual pain. Also administered under doctor's orders were mild sedatives to both parents.

Bobbie Lou said, "We had prayed and prayed, but I don't know how we would have survived if they hadn't done something like that for us. It temporarily took the roughness off of it. When it is your own child, it is really hard."

Welland shared, "We had never had anything serious happen in our family other than a tonsil operation. We had been extremely fortunate the many years we had been married. I think we had grown to feel that nothing adverse could ever happen to us. If you ever feel that way, you want to be careful, because something may happen, and you may be next. We can never be safe in feeling too independent from the Lord.

"I had overcome problems all my life, but I had

never had to face anything like that. It was especially hard for me to accept. I took responsibility for what happened. Remorse and guilt and pent-up emotions were destroying me inside. Nothing had ever tested my faith like this did.

"They had me talk to the floor psychiatrist, and I hated it. She kept pecking at me (I thought) and asking me leading questions, trying to get me to break down and get rid of my emotions. She finally succeeded. I thought she was awful; but I guess she did do a good job. After that I started feeling a little better."

When Natalie returned from surgery, a long hollow tube covered and protected her arm. She couldn't visually see that her hand was gone and many times refused to believe that she had lost it. The sensation that she was holding metal keys returned over and over. "You're just telling me it's gone! I can feel keys; it has to be there!" She would doubt until she drifted off to sleep. But as she awoke, the sensation would be gone, and she would again be forced to accept reality.

The doctors watched the arm closely, and every day as more tissue died the extent of the damage became clearer. Once again, Hansens were required to sign a release for surgery. Their signatures acknowledged they were aware of the risk and gave doctors permission to continue to remove more flesh and muscle. They also knew that complication from the trauma could take Natalie's life, but there was no other choice. With prayer and faith in priesthood blessings, five times in the next three weeks, Natalie would undergo surgery.

Days and sleepless nights rolled into one another as Natalie, just recovering from the last procedure, had to be prepared for the next. Trying to save as much of her arm as possible, the doctors had to keep cutting back the dead tissue until they felt it was stable for the skin grafts. Neither Natalie nor her parents knew of the surgeries until the morning they were performed. Miraculously, as if from heaven itself, after every operation, there were flowers or a special visitor waiting in Natalie's room. Support and love from relatives, friends, and neighbors at home strengthened Natalie and her family through dark days. Concern and support came in visits, cards, and phone calls. Her hospital room was literally wallpapered with tokens of love from so many who cared.

Welland and Bobbie Lou, along with other parents, used the nurses' classroom for a place to be close by and spend sleepless nights. They rested on folded-down chairs and shared the heartache and sorrow of many whose little ones had not only lost hair but also legs from the ravages of cancer. The nurses would come for Bobbie Lou two or three times each night as Natalie would wake and cry. Several amputee survivors came to visit with the children and renew their spirits with true understanding and encouragement.

When the surgeries at last ended and the pins had been removed from the splintered bones, the next step in treatment would be the same as for seriously burned patients. Painful jacuzzi baths would disinfect and remove dead tissue preparing the arm for grafting. Bones, blood vessels, and nerve endings were completely exposed, and up to this point Natalie had never seen her arm. At the beginning of the first treatment she was lightly sedated but as the pill wore off, she recognized her mangled arm and went to pieces. After leaving the recovery room and arriving in her own room, Natalie was calmed by her Aunt Virginia who said, "This is how Heavenly Father created you. Most people never get to see or realize how miraculously everything works under their skin." Natalie began to accept herself and her situation.

When it came time to graft skin over the arm's stub and up to the elbow, the doctors had two options. Their first choice would be to graft Natalie's arm onto her stomach. This would allow a tougher skin layer to develop but would also require another six-week stay in the hospital. Natalie had lost twenty pounds and was extremely weak physically. She had already undergone so much pain and anxiety that her doctors chose the ten-day process of grafting skin from her hips and legs as the best option. However, they warned the Hansens, it was not a sure thing and it may not take.

The removal and the resultant healing of skin patches the size of a large magazine cover from Natalie's legs was her second most painful experience of the entire trauma. The skin over her arm was sewn on just like a piece of cloth with a needle and thread, but even more painful were her raw and stripped legs. A cheese cloth type fabric was laid over them and heat lamps from above added to the discomfort. During that

period, the family prayed continually with deepened
faith and complete trust in the Lord. Welland
recalls,"When you go through a thing like this you
develop a blind faith. You almost have to. You get to a
point where there's nothing concrete that you can
depend on. You live strictly on faith, and naturally
praying continually as we did strengthens your faith."

The moment of truth arrived, and a thrilled
surgeon removed the bandages. It was a perfect graft,
even better than he had hoped. Though the skin was
very thin and there was no feeling in the lower four
inches of her arm, Natalie could go home.

And now a new fear entered Welland and Bobbie
Lou's hearts. How would she adapt? How would she
handle being at home? Bobbie Lou reflected, "We had
worried that of our five children, perhaps it would be
the hardest on Natalie to accept such a situation. Boy,
were we wrong." Still, many heartaches lay ahead.

The first winter Natalie missed a lot of school.
Many days she would call home after only two hours
and need to come home to soak her arm in the jacuzzi
bath that seemed to offer the only relief from pain. How
Bobbie Lou longed for another impossible and
imaginary treatment to heal her daughter's emotional
pain. Bobbie Lou had remained strong in the hospital
when Welland struggled, but now that they had
returned home, the roles had changed and it was a
very difficult time for a mother to witness her
daughter's suffering.

The doctors had warned the adolescent period
was the most critical time in life for losing a limb.

Nearly all of Natalie's friends accepted her and treated her wonderfully, but at times thoughtless peers would make life unbearable. Natalie returned to all of her regular activities including drill team, as she now had an artificial hand to use for performances. Contracting the muscles in her upper arm controlled its fingers, and her greatest challenge was handling the pom-poms. One routine for a half-time show required Natalie to pass the pom-poms over her head to the girl behind her, but she couldn't get the fingers to release. Bobbie Lou watched and agonized from the grandstand as the girl behind pulled and tugged, but Natalie simply couldn't respond with the arm out of control over her head. After the basketball game, heartbroken Natalie was completely devastated as she heard this same girl expressing "her" complete humiliation at being involved in Natalie's problem.

That night after she returned home Bobbie Lou heard muffled sobs from the bedroom. She found Natalie on the floor kneeling next to her bed with blankets over her head sobbing as though her heart would break. Bobbie Lou said, "It hurt me worse than it hurt her, but I didn't let her know it." Instead of focusing on the anger and frustration, she encouraged Natalie to go on. She never offered pity but always said, "Come on, Natalie. You can do it!" She always carried that spirit and motivated Natalie, even though her heart was breaking for her daughter. That strength preserved Natalie through painful days and empty nights when there were no prom invitations, and she felt left out and excluded from social activities.

Another difficult thing for Natalie to overcome during those high school years was jealousy. Natalie recalled saying:

"Why can't I look like so and so? Why can't I have a boyfriend? I even felt occasional jealousy toward my sister, Michelle, whom I loved so much. We were constantly competing with each other. I envied the way she played the piano. (The way I used to be able to.) I had other things to offer, but at the time I couldn't see them. And then Michelle would resent me because she felt Mom and Dad gave me more attention because of the accident. There was a lot of anger and jealousy in high school. I wished desperately that I could change something that I couldn't. It changed a lot as I got a little older and developed a completely different attitude."

But there were many good things during her high school years that came forth from the struggle. Natalie kept a journal every day and expressed and worked through her feelings. Her many poems and thoughts instilled within her deep convictions. She loved the Lord and constantly read good books. wonderful young women leaders and good bishops over the years helped her grow. Several times she was asked to speak to surrounding wards and stakes, and many times it was very difficult for Natalie. "There were times that I didn't want to go," she said. "I didn't feel like I could or that I had enough self esteem or courage. At times I literally had to force myself, but I'm so glad I did. It was really good for me.

"Probably 75% of everything I was able to

accomplish was because my parents were supportive of me in every way. They did everything in their power to help me." Natalie had been a good snow skier and an excellent water skier. The first summer after the accident she learned to pull herself up on one ski with just the strength of her left hand. But she never returned to snow skiing due to the danger of frostbite with no feeling in her lower arm. She had already finished driver's training and had taken typing and was on the freshman gymnastics team. All of those things she quickly relearned to do with her left hand, including gymnastics. She continued to babysit and enjoy little children and they loved her. One of her greatest desires was to continue to play the piano and organ for church, and she did.

A wise and understanding bishop's counselor didn't release her as Jr. Sunday School organist but instead called Michelle to assist her. Each Sunday they would sit side by side and Natalie would play one hand and Michelle the other as sweet music and the spirit of the Lord filled the Sunday School room. Natalie never gave up on her music. She learned to play so beautifully that no one would ever know from listening that she played with just one hand.

Natalie once wrote a short story that reflected her great insight in regards to her accident. When winter comes and a flower or something else you have loved dies, life becomes different than you normally know it. But there is also left room for something else to develop. It may not be a flower, but it may be something else that will grow and take a purpose or maybe even a better purpose.

"That's how I feel about my handicap," she said. "Even though I lost my hand, and it was an interruption in my life, something else just as good, or maybe even better, came along that I could adjust to. There are so many handicaps worse than the one that I have. Some are seen and many are unseen. The Lord gives us each the trials that He thinks we can handle. He knows what we can accomplish with what He has given us."

Natalie had the inner faith to look ahead and find new opportunities for growth.

"I tried out for mascot my senior year. It really scared me because many times that sort of thing is really a popularity contest. But I worked hard and felt I was ready. We had the tryouts, and I didn't make it. One of my really good friends got it, and it was really hard on me. But then it was like the Lord answered my prayers and opened another door. I mustered up all my courage and overcame my fear and inadequacies, and tried out for Jr. Miss."

Every night Natalie practiced long hours perfecting her piano selection. Bobbie Lou listened attentively, and she and Welland quizzed her repeatedly with questions for the judge's conference. Natalie conquered the rigorous physical fitness routine with one arm and finally the day was at hand. A special friend sent flowers and a loving father visited the jewelry store and then presented his beautiful daughter with a diamond and sapphire ring as a token of his love and support. Just going out on the stage that night made Natalie a winner in her family's eyes. Not only did she present herself with poise and confidence, she was selected as second runner-up. What a boost to her self-esteem! It was a new beginning and a new melody in Natalie's life.

The move to college came as an easy adjustment, for Natalie had learned to forget herself and her handicap. She continued to work part-time, just as she had since she was sixteen. During summer vacations in high school, she had been employed as an efficient and competent typist and secretary, first working at the health and welfare offices and then at the medical clinic. As a college student the summer of 1985, Natalie began working at the Utah State University Personnel Services. She is presently the Service Coordinator for the Disabled Students Center on campus. She works capably with approximately eighty students with disabilities. From her, they receive effective and understanding counseling and tutors or proctors to help them adjust to their classes. Natalie's past experience with secretarial and management skills is a great asset in the smooth operation of the center. She is also an advisor for the students' club on campus, IEE (Individuals for Educational Equality).

"I really love my job," she emphatically stated. "My accident has helped me tremendously to help others. I have had many neat experiences." Besides being employed full-time, Natalie calls herself a "professional student" and has taken classes for six years. She plans to graduate with a degree in political science and a minor in business administration.

A couple of years ago, Natalie was invited to return to her home town as a guest speaker at the stake's Debutante Ball. Before the girls were presented by their fathers to the audience, they gathered in a beautifully decorated room for instruction. Seated in their lovely gowns, each young woman's heart was touched by Natalie's profound message. A beautiful spirit filled the room as Natalie shared how after losing her hand, she didn't feel very pretty or good about herself. She decided the thing to do was to work on what was inside, where it really counted. Her accident and physical loss made her try to be the person she felt she needed to be.

She was indeed beautiful, not only on the outside, but deep within. That beauty was immediately noticed and appreciated by Jason Sterling, a handsome young man and special friend to Natalie in Logan. They had known each other for nearly two years when their friendship blossomed into love. Their courtship prepared them for another unforgettable autumn day, some ten years after Natalie's accident. On October 28, 1988, Natalie and Jason were sealed as husband and wife in the LDS Logan Temple.

As a beautiful and radiant bride whose life rings sweetly with the melody of love and conviction, Natalie has prepared herself to be a light and inspiration to others. She still faces "phantom pain," and "feels" her missing hand, as her delicately healed arm has been broken four times, and she lives with painful bone spurs and frequent infections. But as she meets each day's challenges, she develops an increased understanding of others and the "gift" to see their needs. Her own trials have developed within her the ability to reach out to others.

"I've really always tried not to look at it as a handicap, but to look at it as an asset," Natalie commented, "something that I can use not only to help myself develop good qualities, but also to help other people.

"I know I can do whatever I need to do. My patriarchal blessing promises, as long as I'm doing right, regardless of what it is, if I'm bound and determined, I can succeed. My righteous desires will come forth.

"Many times I have contemplated that when I see Heavenly Father again, I will have my hand. That's really encouraging to me. This is just one step in my eternal life."

CHAPTER FOUR

Silent Warrior

Garth

Amid the constant talk of war, the days of youth were carefree for young, teen-age Garth. Sports, especially football, were his greatest love and life was happy and fairly simple. He and his friends' group dated to the stake dances. Few had cars, and whoever could get the family car would "pick up" everyone along the way and then deliver them home. Although all the girls had dance programs, each was expected to save the first, middle, and last dance for her partner. The "Wandamere" dance pavilion in Idaho Falls was the "hot spot" where you could dance to live music featuring the latest hits of the big name bands. Toes tapped, and couples jitterbugged to the sounds of Glenn Miller's "In the Mood" and "String of Pearls" and

Tommy Dorsey's "Boogie Woogie."

That youthful idyll was very fragile, however, as political forces were moving to a point where they would one day clash and shatter the peaceful simplicity that Garth Thompson and other young men like him had once known.

In the early 1940s, Japan was an expansionist power and the more aggressive it was to China, the more it outraged the United States. America's paternal attitude towards China was combined with a fear of Japan as a naval rival and a potential threat to the American west coast.

Radio newscasters predicted that war was imminent and at the "back door of the United States." And the United States reacted by speeding up its expansion of military and industrial facilities and increasing its armed forces.

Conscription through legislation became the law in September 1940, providing individual draft boards in each county. Registration for the draft began immediately for all unmarried males 21 and over. The boards tried to prioritize calls. Those whose service would create the least hardship at home were the ones selected first.

It happened—December 7, 1941. Even though their official envoys were still negotiating in Washington, D.C., the Japanese attacked Pearl Harbor, the Philippines, Guam, Midway, Hong Kong, and Malaysia. Although these were small islands, they were crucial for air combat. Americans were devastated. U. S. Naval losses at Pearl Harbor were of near-catastrophic proportions.

Monday morning, December 8, 1941, Franklin Delano Roosevelt, President of the United States, addressed the joint session of Congress and asked it to declare war on the Axis powers. Garth, along with thousands of other Americans, clustered around the radio to hear President Roosevelt declare "America must remain an arsenal of democracy." The fears of all Americans, as well as that of a young country boy, had become a reality. America was in World War II.

Hundreds of thousands of young men rushed to join the different branches of service to do "their duty to their country." Those who were unable to pass physicals for the armed service found other means to serve. Defense plants opened, and men and women went to work building whatever was necessary to keep the fighting men going.

Family Interruption

At seventeen, Garth, filled with youthful patriotic zeal, would have rushed to find a way to serve his country. But war was pushed to the back of his mind as he struggled with an "interruption" in the even tenure of his life closer to home. It was a terrible blow for Garth when his parents were in an automobile accident which severely injured both of them. Doctors said they would never be able to work again.

Garth was the oldest, so there was no question in his mind as to who would assume responsibility for the family. He took over the farm, making all the decisions for its maintenance, thus providing for the needs of his siblings (one sister and two brothers) and his parents. Now the bread-winner was pitched headlong into heavy responsibilities light years away from carefree teenage pursuits. Garth wanted to be a good farmer, not only for himself, but for his family and country. He had heard the saying, "An army travels on its stomach," and Garth was determined to help supply food for the men who had willingly consented to protect his country.

The transition from boy to man is not easily seen as it occurs, but Garth, the boy, took on the responsibilities of his father, and the transition to manhood began.

There were many decisions to be made in the spring of 1942. Garth was now the one to determine the planting and irrigation, and he was responsible to bring in a good harvest.

Still, not all of Garth's attention rested with farming. He had to forego his first love, sports, due to lack of time, but he still had time to attend the socials. When the seminary party was announced, he invited beautiful, blond Winona Searle, and soon he realized he'd found a worthy replacement for his first love. Winona had been dating Garth's good friend, but after the party she only had eyes for Garth. After her junior year in high school, she was certain this honest, good-looking boy who always treated her like a lady was the one she wanted to spend her life with.

But even while Garth's life was full of farm

work, school, friends, and doing his "bit" at home, he knew the time was soon at hand when he would be old enough to be summoned to war.

War on the Home Front

Garth saw evidence all around him that the war was accelerating. The United States was in the heat of battle. Each man, woman, and child on the home front was doing everything possible to contribute to the war effort. Rationing of goods was commonplace. Everyone had rationing stamp books, one for each member of their family. Shoes, sugar, meat, butter, and shortening could only be purchased with a ration stamp accompanying the money. The phrase "Fill it up" was no longer recognized at gas stations.

Still everyone sought to do his part. War Bond and Savings Stamp drives were held. Boy Scouts were organized with the Civil Defense, carrying out air raid practices, preparing the public in case of a dreaded attack. The air waves were filled with music to lighten the heart and enhance the soul with patriotism. Songs like "Comin' in on a Wing and a Prayer" and "Don't Sit under the Apple tree with Anyone Else but Me" were listened to, danced to, and cherished.

Hanging in the window of many homes was a small service flag with a blue star for each family member in the armed forces. When the worst happened and word came from the War Department telling of a loved one's death, the blue star was changed to gold.

Casualty lists were printed in the newspaper naming the war dead and those wounded or missing in action. The faces of the dead and missing men stared back from the front page.

The war had seemed so far away and unreal, fought abroad by unknown men. But now it was real, and the casualty lists were growing. Those who were dying were fathers, husbands, sons, and even the young boy who bagged your groceries at the local store every Saturday. Strangers, neighbors, friends, and loved ones clung together for a single cause.

And still the war continued to escalate. In Europe, the dictator Hitler was consumed with his hatred of the Jews and his desire to rule the world at all costs. The shooting of hostages in retaliation for almost any hostile act toward the Germans became commonplace. Never had the world seen such a cold and calculated campaign of terrorism and cruelty.

In the Pacific, the Philippine Islands were a logical objective for both military and political reasons. These islands and surrounding islands, although small, were needed by the U.S. for air combat. General Douglas MacArthur had landed in Leyte and invaded the Philippines by May of 1944.

The war still seemed pretty far away to Garth Thompson. There was so much for him to be concerned with at home with his parents' poor health and farming problems, but he struggled with the question of what would happen to his parents when his call to serve came. He knew his brothers and sister would remain at home, but it was still a grave concern.

What about the farm? What about his country? what about Winona? he repeatedly asked himself.

Garth was twenty now, and as soon as the crops were harvested, he would have to leave to serve his country. Despite the worries over his family, Garth wanted to serve. He remembered thinking, "We must not, we will not, let our freedom, the liberty and the things we hold dear, be taken from us by oppressors. Maybe I can help in some way."

In October, Garth was inducted into the army as a "foot soldier." Little did he realize that before another year was over he would be in hand-to-hand combat in the Philippines.

The solemnity of it all but overtook him the day he left his loved ones behind. He wondered, "When will I see my home and family again?" How he would endure it all was a question only time could answer.

Garth had never been very far from home, so there was much in store for a young man straight from the farm in Idaho. He was sent to Camp Walters, Texas, for basic training, and *training* it was. Army discipline taught him to stay alive if possible and to destroy the enemy. Garth valued life and had no desire to lose his life or anyone else's. But he knew his country was under attack and he was willing to give his life, if necessary, and do anything required to protect and preserve freedom for the future he hoped to have.

Life changed with basic training, and Garth functioned on military time. He learned to do as he was told, to rap out "Sir" to salute officers, and to instantly obey a command. He couldn't have foreseen that "basic training" would instill automatic responses that would one day save his life.

This raw recruit would learn to study hard and listen as he had never listened before. He would learn the in's and out's of weapons until they would seem like an appendage of his own body.

Basic training also served to test Garth's religious convictions. Although there were some who did not understand or show tolerance for his religion, Garth stayed true to those things he knew to be right, and the blessing of protection was his.

Basic training was over in February, 1945, and Winona and a friend visited Garth in Texas. He knew then he would someday marry her. Later, when Garth got a five-day furlough, he knew it wasn't much time to get home to Idaho and convince "his girl," but he had marriage on his mind. With two other fellows from Idaho, he found a ride home, making the trip in one-and-half days. As soon as he arrived home, he went to the store where Winona worked and at closing time asked the question, "Are we going to get married?" Her answer was as he had hoped.

The young couple knew time was short, and yet something so precious as their wedding had to be right. Their future was uncertain, but they were in love in spite of the war. So many had fatalistic attitudes, but they would not let the mustached dictator in Europe destroy their hopes and dreams of a better life.

Garth knew the importance of prayer and living

the commandments. His long-range view of life made him realize life should not be lived carelessly but with purpose and direction. And the direction Garth and Winona knew they should take was to the Salt Lake Temple. Whatever the outcome in the uncertainty of life, they felt the best reinforcement was to start their life together in the House of the Lord.

When they went into the County Building to obtain their marriage license, Garth's mother went along to give her permission. Garth lacked the right change for the license, so Winona paid for it. The memory of their temple marriage would bring much joy to each of them when the uncertainties of life crowded in. They left the temple of God, that Friday, March 2, 1945, married for time and eternity. And regardless of what the circumstances of war would bring, they had the assurance that the plan of God would never fail.

The following Tuesday Garth left for Fort Ord, California, and then to parts unknown. His imagination could not fathom the challenges that lay ahead.

Boarded on the troop ship, the *H.S. Sturges*, were 5,000 troops and 33 officers. There was no escort ship so the *Sturges* zig-zagged across the Pacific. Garth was no longer in charge of his own itinerary; now he would go where he was sent. Those far-off places mentioned on the Gabriel Heater news broadcast would soon become locations and situations that would be indelibly imprinted on his mind. Garth would experience another interruption—another dimension—to manhood.

Life in the Pacific

The first land Garth saw after leaving California was Guadacanal. The *Sturges* maneuvered through the strait and landed in New Guinea, picking up a convoy and heading for Manila to replace battle-worn troops.

The harbor was full of sunken ships, and the fighting was intense street-to-street. As Garth said, "For an old country boy who had never been anywhere in the world, it was quite a shock."

The ship couldn't get into the harbor, so the men had to climb down over the side on nets and wade ashore. From there they were loaded into trucks and taken out into rice fields to pitch their tents. In this strange country were things Garth had only read about and never seen. Everywhere were fruit-laden banana trees and other curious-looking fruits.

Guards placed around the perimeter of camp were the first indication that the enemy was very near. Now as the young men faced the reality of the enemy, each heart wondered if it had learned its lessons well.

The next morning the troops were lined up alphabetically and assigned to different divisions. In the 38th Division, there was only one man Garth knew, an eighteen-year-old, "Van Kirk" from Weiser, Idaho.

Once again, the soldiers were loaded on trucks and taken to the Mariveles Valley, a large plain of rice paddies, banana groves, and pineapple fields which had almost grown wild. This was the front of the line. They were to hold back the Japanese, who had been pushed into the hills above the valley. As they got off the truck in the middle of the afternoon, they saw what had once been beautiful homes and profitable farms owned by wealthy landowners, now destroyed by the ravages of war.

That night K.P.'s were brought in to prepare a hot meal. This was a rare occasion, as most of the time the men lived on "C" rations.

Garth was assigned to the 151st Regiment which was a National Guard unit from Indiana. This regiment had been called up at the beginning of the war and some of the men, as old as forty, had been in active duty as long as five years. Garth said, "Some of them were unable to write their names and had to sign with an X. But could they fight!" A regiment, consisting of approximately 3,000 men, was broken down into battalions, companies, platoons, and squads.

Garth related the following about his first day in the Mariveles Valley:

"When we first arrived in the valley, a man who spoke with authority said as he pointed over to some banana trees, 'You are attached to my squad—start digging your foxhole!' As he walked off, he threw over his shoulder, 'I'll be back with some weapons for you.' When he came back, he was dragging 50-calibre machine guns. I had never seen one before."

"I don't know how to use one of these guns," I quickly told him.

"Nothing to it!" he snapped curtly. "If you hear

something out here tonight just point the gun in front of you, pull back the crank, and hang on."

"We got ambushed that night. Only four months from home, and I was in the thick of reality."

The Mariveles River flowed down through the valley, with the Americans on one side and the enemy on the other. With the first light of morning, the squad went on patrol down the river.

Because of the heat, each man carried two canteens. One man would walk out into the water about half way, fill his canteens, and drop in two halazone tablets to purify the water. When he had reached the other side, another man would jump in, and the procedure would continue until all the men had crossed the river pursuing the enemy.

During Garth's first day on the fighting lines, they encountered no resistance, and he returned to the same foxhole which he shared with another soldier. With two in the same foxhole, they could hopefully alternate between sleep and keeping watch. Garth said, "The senses became finely tuned to anything out of the ordinary, so at first when a long python snake slithered next to me, his presence was rather alarming. But I soon learned he was only looking for a warm place where he could cuddle against the chilly night, and our intruder was left undisturbed."

It was hot and muggy in the daytime, and it got very chilly at night. After the sun went down, a mist would rise from the ground. The soldiers' boots would be green with mold the next morning, and their clothing would rot out at the seams. The much-needed weapons were a concern. When supplies arrived, all guns with the first sign of rusting would be "chucked," and a new one would be issued. Every precaution was taken for protection against the enemy.

Garth recalled, "We had just gotten into our foxholes that first night when trucks kept coming and going. The next morning we saw piles of guns, radios, grenades, and some beer rations. Since I didn't drink beer, there were several that were happy to receive my quota. Some of the guys wanted the beer so badly they discarded their ammunition clips so they could pack more beer with them.

"I really wondered what we were getting into. Every man's lifestyle was different, and it was something you respected. However, it did leave room for concern, because in combat every faculty a person has needs to be alert. There's no margin for error." Regardless of their religious affiliation, there were no unbelievers in the foxholes.

Garth had only begun in this seemingly forsaken land and already he wondered if there would ever be anything else. Again he prayed for strength to do what had to be done. Home seemed a million miles away.

The next morning they crossed the river and never returned. They just went forward.

The troops pressed forward south and east of the Battaan Peninsula at the lower end of the Philippines. The territory was encased in huge vines hanging everywhere with tall waist-high elephant grass. They walked single file with eyes ahead, alert, and listening for any sound that would let them know the enemy was near. Rifles were held secure and high above their heads. Garth said they were taught, "You never know where the enemy is until they decide to shoot at you."

An officer with a whiplash voice and seemingly arrogant way in the United States was not easily recognized in the jungles of war in the Philippines. Although respect for an officer was assumed, these men were now companions in battle, and everyone looked the same in army fatigues. The unimportant was stripped away, and they only saw each other's true worth.

Fear of a sniper's bullet and the palatable delight of the enemy to "get an American officer" caused the officers not to wear their insignias. You had to remember which ones were officers. Or at least you tried to.

Garth recalls his squad edging their way through elephant grass and bamboo. It was essential to keep noise at a minimum. The sergeant in charge heard more noise than he thought necessary.

"Don't you know how to move, soldier? The enemy could be anywhere!" the sergeant "quietly" yelled, straining his voice to make his point, but still not alerting the enemy himself.

"What are you trying to do, get us all killed?" He aimed his glare at the red-headed soldier.

"Can you quiet down, or do I have to show you how?"

"I can handle it," came the self-assured reply.

"You had better make _____ sure you do!

What's your rank?"

"Full Colonel, Sergeant."

With a little less enthusiasm, the sergeant coughed and with a wry smile said, "Thank you, Sir!"

The role of the foot soldier was one of hanging on, of driving from the mind what the next five minutes may bring. The sounds of war resounded everywhere, and the past slipped into the shadows.

To recapture each day-to-day experience is impossible. The memory seeks to elude the horror where possible. Garth, the young farm boy, was now a man, married, and fighting for a future. During the next six weeks, he would often question the interruptions in his life.

Early one morning Garth was assigned as first scout for the platoon. The scouts led the way and radioed back the signal when and where to fire to the mortar and machine gun squads following. Philippine laborers, hired to help carry supplies and bring back the dead and wounded on stretchers, accompanied them.

"Thompson, fall back," the staff sergeant roared. "Let Vackie take your place."

Garth had learned from the early days of boot camp to instantly obey an order. He recalled:

"There was a little stream of water right by me. I bent over to fill my canteen and then I stepped back to let Vackie through. Because of the heavy growth and brush, I had to step up and to one side to let him pass. Just as he approached my place a round of ammunition went off. They hit Vackie five times, and he fell back into my arms."

Another time, in another place, an officer was inspecting the front lines in a no-man's land.

"Do you see them? Do you see them, son?" he quietly asked one of the recruits who stood guard in the darkness.

"See who, sir? I can't see anyone," the puzzled young man answered.

The older man, experienced in the hazards of war, replied, "Your buddies, son. Your buddies who died today and yesterday. They are out there watching us, wondering what we are going to do, wondering if they died in vain."

Garth was consumed in thoughts of what had happened that day. "Why? Why Vackie, and not me?" He started blankly into the eerie night. "Are you there, Vackie? Are you there?"

Heavy artillery was brought in, a path was cleared, and pursuit of the enemy continued. Four days later the American soldiers came out of the jungle and approached a hill. They walked in single file about four feet apart. As they reached the brow of the hill, the enemy opened up woodpecker, which produced short bursts of gunfire.

VanKirk, an eighteen-year-old boy from Weiser, Idaho, and Garth's good friend since entering the service, was hit in the stomach.

"It was terrible," remembered Garth. "I yelled for the medic, and he jumped on his legs. I got on his head, and we held him down while the medic gave him a shot of pure morphine. That knocked him out until we could get more help. Just as he finished the injection, the enemy opened fire again and hit the medic in the buttocks."

With more courage than foresight, Garth acted. "I jumped up and pulled them both over the hill to the other side, out of the range of fire and yelled for another medic. VanKirk was loaded on a stretcher, but on the way out to a medical station, he died.

"This was my good friend. We had been through it all together. I had known him since boot camp. Why? Why?" The question repeated itself over and over in Garth's mind, but there would be no answer.

While Garth was suffering the pain of his friend's death, at home his first son, Larry, was being born. He would not learn of it until a month later.

A week after his young friend died, the composition of the squads was changed, and Garth was again assigned as scout.

The fighting was more fierce and more intense. He and four others were equipped with Thompson submachine guns. As they edged their way through the thick jungle, they "sprayed the air" at the first sign of movement. It was shoot first or be killed. The machine guns were more effective and considerably faster than the rifle, but in only four short days even more fire power was needed.

The BAR (Browning Automatic Rifle) shot clips, about twenty shots at a time with one pull of the trigger. But this gun took more ammunition. The "ammo" bearers walked one in front and one behind the man with the BAR. They each wore jackets similar to fishing jackets, with big pockets to carry the ammo clips.

From a better vantage point that night Garth's unit dug their foxholes near the top of a hill. The night passed with little disturbance or close range firing. In the distance, flashes of light and loud explosions filled the sky like the 4th of July. No rest or relief came. After such intensive days, the night seemed almost too calm.

The next morning as they started over the hill, they could see a clearing, a little valley below about the size of three or four acres, and a well-defined trail which wound back into the jungle on the other side of the valley. A reconnaissance group had already gone ahead. Just as they made their descent about a fourth of the way down, the reconnaissance group met with resistance and started firing. Only then did they realize the trap. The enemy had them in cross-fire. It was an ambush! The enemy's well-laid plan worked!

"Everywhere you looked tracers were flying and whizzing past," Garth said. "I ran all my clips through my gun. I looked ahead and saw Martinez fall. As I turned around, the fellow behind me was going down. I kept looking, and I realized I was the only one left. Everywhere I turned, I saw death. I was so stunned and confused; my senses were reeling.

"A Polish fellow who played professional baseball for the Philadelphia Phillies, called to me, and when I didn't respond, he grabbed me and said, 'Thompson, let's get the ___ out of here.' We took off through the bush and got back to the rest of our company. The artillery had to take over from there."

Garth would contemplate for a long time to come the experiences of that day. He now knew the cliche "hair stood on ends" was more than a joke. It was real.

The cry of "why me?" so often reaches the lips of those suffering tragedy. But Garth who had been born in the little farming community of Woodville, Idaho, and received his initiation into manhood on the battlefront of the Philippines, also asked, "Why me? Why am I still alive? Why am I so blessed?" Death stared him in the face on every turn; his buddies were all gone; and yet he was alive. "I can only think the Lord has his finger on me for something." For some reason his life had been spared—for what he knew not; but this he did know, it would not be in vain.

The U.S. Sixth Army moved to the main island of Luzon, and in January of 1945 they began a drive down the central plains toward Manila. The Japanese, under General Yamashita, fought hard to defend Manila. Nevertheless, by March, Manila was liberated, although virtually demolished. Its bay was soon open to Allied shipping. At the same time, a force equivalent to twelve divisions, the largest to fight in any single ground campaign of the Pacific, was built up against General Yamashita's mountain strongholds. The Japanese defended tenaciously from a labyrinth of caves. They had an arsenal of protection, with guns mounted in concrete bunkers from the dams. It seemed virtually impossible for the American soldiers to get through. U.S. tanks were sent in only to be literally blown off the road. For the first time, American forces were outnumbered.

After the American rescue of Saipan and Guadacanal, an air base was set up. Garth remembered, "This was the first time I had seen planes in combat." First came the B-26 two-engine light bombers that dropped bombs on parachutes. They would go down to twenty or thirty feet off the ground and explode, causing huge ebony hardwood trees to disintegrate like matchsticks.

The P-47 fighter planes arrived, and on their wings were Napon bombs or cylinders filled with jelly gasoline. When they hit the ground, the whole thing exploded and fire consumed everything in sight.

The Japanese were well-acquainted with the terrain and could "hole up" in the network of caves that protected them from the enormity of the bombs. But time was no longer on their side. Now they were running out of ammunition and food. They were cut off from their homeland, and their only source of existence now was the "C" rations scavenged from the Americans and what fruit they could find on wild banana trees.

Garth remembered thinking, "They were the enemy, but it was hard to think of them starving to death. They were fighting for their country just as we were fighting for ours."

The language of war was everywhere and the stench of death reduced the appetite. All they had were "C" rations parachuted into them. They were hardly savory to the taste, but at least helped the men stay alive. The body moved and did what had to be done, but the mind refused to ruminate the tragedy surrounding them.

The days and nights were endless, one only being recognized by the light of day or the dark of night. Sometime in June, Garth and the men with him were "dug-down" in a foxhole near the top of a hill. They watched and waited.

It was 4 p.m. and the heat of the day was exhausting. From all sides, the caves seemed to come alive with loud noise, pans rattling, people screaming and charging with bayonets—a "last resort" to destroy the Americans.

Even though basic training had trained and disciplined these G.I.'s to fight and kill, when they saw starving, desperate people, banging pans and anything else they could find to throw off the enemy, they were almost too stunned to move. The Americans outnumbered the Japanese now, and through this last desperate effort many lives were lost.

"To have a man come at you with a bayonet, a knife or a gun, not caring if he lives or dies, gives you a lot to think about," Garth recalled, with tears and sadness. He could only wonder how to stop someone who did not care if he lived or died and not lose his own life in the attempt.

Though death was still imminent on all sides, it was finally the beginning of the end.

Garth said, "That night we got shelled good. Mortar rounds and machine-gun fire was everywhere. Some of the mortar hit a tree and exploded, and I was hit in the leg. After they put me on a stretcher, it took them two days to get me out.

"The Philippine stretcher bearers would sweat and strain to try and keep me as comfortable as possible. Finally we got to a Catholic monastery outside Manila that had been made into a makeshift hospital. There surgery was performed, and I could get relief from the pain. I was out of the war six weeks."

After Garth was released and strong enough to go back to his company, things were winding up. Now two or three men would be sent to an outpost along with fifty or sixty Philippine soldiers in their command. Every day one of them would take some of the Philippine soldiers and go out in dangerous search of the enemy.

The tension mounted, life was still very much on the line and the patrol leaders were the obvious target. The performance of each squad was measured in life and death.

Discipline and order are most effective tools in saving lives. However, on the battle front, the officers and recruits are just men, and buddies. The bond of friendship that begins there in the midst of crisis is not easily extinguished or withered by time.

As America's forces were becoming stronger, kamikaze (suicide) planes were the enemy's only hope of defeating the big Allied fleet standing offshore. Although the Japanese sank about 25 ships, their desperate attacks failed to stop U.S. troops on Okinawa, only 700 miles southwest of Japan. This was the last invasion before "hitting" the homelands of Japan.

By midsummer of 1945, the most responsible leaders in Japan recognized that the end was near.

They accepted Allied peace terms on August 14, and the next day August 15, was proclaimed V-J Day. Formal surrender documents were signed aboard the *USS Missouri* in Tokyo Bay on September 2, bringing World War II to an end. Garth still remembers the joyful feeling he experienced when the announcement came, "The war is over!"

The Aftermath

Although the war was over, home was still a long way off. Every serviceman was given points and returned home according to the number of points he had. To be married with a son doubled Garth's points; however, it would still be another year before he saw American soil.

Garth was assigned to detached service discharging the Philippine guerrilla army. He was a medical corpsman and gave physicals before the men were discharged. Some of them had never seen a doctor as they lived and died in the little barrios called home.

Garth would again question his life. Why was he born in America with its freedom and privileges completely lacking in this land of the Philippines? He gave much thought concerning life and its purpose, and the young soldier vowed to live as his Creator intended.

It was Garth's responsibility to be in charge of one of the depots and oversee work details that kept the Japanese prisoners of war occupied. Japanese officers took total responsibility for the conduct of their men. Garth did not have to answer bugle call and one morning when a truckload of prisoners arrived, two men jumped off the truck and came into his barracks, grabbed his pants and held them up to help him dress. These proud men now took the part of the servant. Garth felt, "I could never be a servant to another nation or philosophy or bow to another, but at the same time I could not allow another human being to be a servant to me." The war was over, and although they were prisoners, they would still be treated as human beings. Garth begrudged no man and carried with him the knowledge that it was not his brother or another people who were his enemy, but enslavement and false ideologies.

"I didn't hold any animosity to those people. The longer I was with them, the more I knew I had a great deal in common with them. One of the officers had graduated from a university in Japan in agriculture. He was just like me. He liked the same things, and I'm sure he loved country and family the same that I did."

Going Home

At last, the time had come. It was August, 1946, and Garth was going home. He would leave the land where death and bloodshed had become commonplace. In the stillness of night, he thought about his buddies who would not be going home. On the return trip across the Pacific, he wondered how difficult the adjustment to home would be.

CHAPTER FIVE

Stepping Into Eternity

Rachelle

"Her life here was a brief interruption in her Eternal Progression."

A well-known philosopher recently asked if we could see ourselves as spiritual beings having a mortal experience, rather than mortal beings trying to have an occasional spiritual experience. As we come to see more clearly that we are literally living each and every day in the midst of eternity, life's experiences become more meaningful.

It was a typical, crisp Sunday morning in mid-September, and school had just been dismissed for potato harvest. Two weeks of anticipated freedom lay ahead, and pent-up energies made church seem long in the Pingree 2nd Ward.

That morning in the Course 13 Sunday School class the substitute teacher gave a lesson on Christ's last week on the earth. She taught that the Savior showed love and rendered service to those around Him, as He surely realized His time was short.

Then she asked the class, "What would it be like to know you only had one week left to live? What would you do?" The class laughed and joked, full of humor and early teen mischief. One handsome lad said he would definitely go on a date because he would never get a chance later. All but one giggled and joined in the fun as the teacher called on each student to respond. Gaiety and excitement of unfulfilled youth permeated the classroom until it became the turn of a pretty and very popular, dark-haired girl who had sat silently on the front row.

"That isn't what I would do," she quietly said. Everyone turned to listen, as this was the first comment she had made during the entire lesson. Immediately sensing the spirit carried by this serene and thoughtful girl, the teacher responded, "What would you do, Rachelle?" as she looked into the depth of young, but mature, understanding eyes.

"I would tell my mother that I love her, and I would spend as much time with my family as I could because they are my best friends."

The room became silent. There was no comeback from the boys. The girls looked at the floor. All were quiet and humbled as they realized that Rachelle had really considered what it would be like to leave this life in one week. The uncomfortable reverence was broken with the ringing of the bell. A closing prayer was offered, and off they went, perhaps not giving another thought to the discussion until the shocking news came not quite a week later. Rachelle had thought about life, and what eternity would be like. Six days later she would see it clearly.

"The highest reward for man's toil is not what he gets for it but what he becomes by it." John Ruskin.
The next few days proved long and grueling, as this "two-week vacation" usually is. The tedious job of picking clods on a potato combine begins early every morning and ends well after dark. But the chance to work is eagerly coveted by the area's youth, enabling them to make substantial earnings to offset school expenses and save for missions and college. Perhaps greater than financial gain is the opportunity to test personal discipline and to strengthen character by seeing an "endless" and very difficult task completed. Harvest is especially rewarding when one gets to work with family and friends as Rachelle did the harvest of 1987. The farmer she worked for was a dear and close neighbor who was willing to give dependable young people a chance to work. On the crew were cousins and Rachelle's older brother and sister, Clint, a junior, and JaNae, a freshman in high school. Good friends from junior high were also in the field, and the conversation usually centered around school activities and girls' basketball tryouts after harvest.

Rachelle's exuberance for life was evident in her love of sports. As a guard on the basketball team, she delighted many as she enthusiastically dribbled down the court with the ball that occasionally got out of control. Such mistakes never daunted Rachelle's spirit. She was right back in the game, smiling it off, and giving it her all, as she did in every challenge. As an A student, she qualified for Honor Society and was elected secretary. She had served as seventh grade class vice-president, and when school resumed she planned to run for studentbody office. This fall was her first semester in eighth grade, and she was one of the star players on the girls' volleyball team.

In addition to her skill on a ball court or in competition, Rachelle carried within an upward reach. She saw others at their best and wanted them to view themselves the same way. She seemed to have a yearning for sublimity in everyday life. But things did not always come easily to Rachelle. Persistence and hard work which seemed second nature usually concealed to the public eye the fears and anxieties she shared with most young people her age.

You see youth as a joyous thing
About whom love and laughter cling.
You see youth as a joyful elf
Who sings sweet songs to please himself.
You see his laughing, sparkling eyes
To take earth's wonders with surprise.
You think him free from cares and woes
And naught of fear you think he knows,
You see him thus, for you are old.

But I, I see him otherwise
An unknown fear lies in his eyes
He works and plays and never knows,
Where he is called nor why he goes.
Each youth sustains within his breast
A vague and infinite unrest.
He goes about in still alarm,
With shrouded future at his arm,
With longings that can find no tongue.
I see him thus, for I am young. [1]

The evening before school was to start in the seventh grade, Rachelle felt the weight of the "shrouded future" and turned to her mother's arms. Great were the anxieties of entering a new school. Would she fit in? Would she be accepted? She tearfully acknowledged her fears and then shared with her Mom a little notebook in which she had planned and written a list of every outfit she would wear for the next week. After finding the confidence and encouragement she needed, she emerged the next day at school, smiling, poised, and confident, appearing not to have a care in the world. How delighted and pleased her mother was when she came home beaming. No one outside her home knew of her personal trial and fear, and yet she carried with dignity the insecurity of being

---

[1] Author unknown-Cheryl LeBaron, *Becoming All That You Are* (Salt Lake City, UT, RIC Publishing, 1982) p. 1.

thirteen.

Rachelle had developed an inner strength early in life. Many times she would be in the house studying as playmates' laughter filtered through the screen door. She had a great desire to play the piano, but it just didn't seem to come naturally. So once again determination took over. On busy days she would come charging through the house, stop momentarily to play her piece as perfectly as she could and then be on her way, stopping later in the day for a repeat performance. Rachelle had a natural knack for knowing what needed to be done and then doing it, usually without being asked. If she especially disliked a job, like mowing the lawn, she would tear into it working relentlessly until she had her section done, and she was usually the first finished. But all these things had been set aside for now, the work at hand was potato harvest. Everything comes to a stop during potato harvest, even Young Women activities.

"My Way"

Rachelle especially loved her Beehive teacher, Susan, who at camp a couple of months earlier had been her secret pal. What fun to have an advisor who was also a special friend! Little did Rachelle know that Susan wondered many times as they shared confidences and set goals in personal progress interviews, if she were looking into the eyes of a thirteen-year-old. Or was it a more mature reflection of an eighteen-year-old young woman that returned her gaze? Susan admired her beauty and grace, with never a hair out of place. She was a pretty, eye-catching beauty, but she never set herself apart from others. Instead, she had the ability to make others feel accepted. Her sweet disposition made everyone feel that she was their friend.

Susan learned that Rachelle would always reach the goals she set for herself even if they proved difficult, and then she would select a new challenge. As she stood every Sunday and repeated with her friends, "We are daughters of a Heavenly Father who loves us and we love him," Susan would see the conviction in her face. In class, her intent look indicated she was trying to grasp and remember every word. Reading the Book of Mormon and praying were part of her daily schedule. Rachelle carried her convictions through the week as she had the courage to be herself and determine her own pace and direction. She dressed modestly and set her own style, including her "neon leons" for shoelaces.

The Sunday before harvest began, Rachelle sat on the toy box in her newly redecorated bedroom and admired the soft pink walls and grey trim which she had completely painted herself. How proud she was at how well it was coming together. She and her younger sister, Lorraine, now in the seventh grade, would share this special sanctuary together. Just last month they had gone through all of Rachelle's boxed treasures stored in the front room closet, and she explained what each meant and shared many with Lorraine.

The Hall family had been extensively remodelling all summer, doing most of the work themselves, with Clint and the girls even helping shingle the roof—an enormous task they completed in one day. Sure-footed Rachelle and her sisters would lay out the shingles, and Clint and his Dad would nail them in place.

Until now, the three girls, just a year apart, had always shared a room. They had had their spats, and yet they remained close and united. When Lorraine was afraid on the top bunk at night, Rachelle would reach up and hold her hand until she felt safe enough to fall asleep. Even though JaNae was a year older, she always found her sister willing to talk and comfort her in her trials. Many times Rachelle wrapped understanding arms around trembling shoulders and shared her tears. "Just be the best you can be. Don't worry about others; it doesn't matter, just be you," was the counsel given by a young girl. At the end of such sessions, she would always return and put her head inside the door to say, "I love you, JaNae." And Clint, the oldest and the only boy and naturally the strongest, would appreciate Rachelle's staying up until early morning hours when he needed a friend and someone to trust. They were a handsome bunch. Stuart had been ward clerk for six years and felt great pride as he watched his companion and beautiful children from the stand in church.

This weekend Joan had helped Rachelle wallpaper her room. An uncooperative corner caused great distress as a tired mother couldn't make the seam fit just right. When Joan became upset, Rachelle looked at her with deep understanding eyes and said, "It's all right, Mom. You don't have to do it today if it upsets you." But being determined, as all mothers are, Joan finished the wall and Rachelle was so pleased and proud. She had paid for her own daybed, and with her harvest money she could buy the carpet she had chosen.

The Halls recognized their daughter was more mature than her natural years, and when Rachelle was a small child, Joan sensed "she was a grown spirit trapped in a little body as though she couldn't wait to grow up and get on with things." Her keen intellect and deep perception made her appear that "she could hardly wait for the next experience in life." Just that summer, Joan had told her mother as they visited in Washington where Rachelle had tended little cousins for six weeks, "I don't know if I will ever raise Rachelle because she is getting so perfect." Rachelle had had a couple of serious injuries earlier on, but this feeling was different. "She was like a grown woman in a young girl's body." Sometimes I would look into her eyes when I had done something wrong or handled a situation inappropriately, and I felt her silent but loving pleading, "Mom, why do you do that?" This child peacemaker continually sought to make life better. She carried peace and sweetness next door to Grandma and Grandpa's house, too. Quietly she would slip in and snuggle on the couch by Grandpa, who had been in failing health, or sit next to Grandma Dona as she sewed beautiful holiday dresses for the girls. Little did she know she was uniting her family for eternity.

Rachelle seemed to have a special insight and ability to judge things for herself. The only "no's" Stuart and Joan had to give were those limiting the number of activities Rachelle took part in. She wanted to learn to do everything, and as with all families, there had to be limits. When she was told no, she accepted their judgment. "We hardly ever had to say no. But when we did, we never had to repeat it."

One day rolled into another this harvest week. Stuart worked each evening after work on the house, feeling strangely compelled to get finished. Joan had been keyed up all month, feeling as though she would explode, but when Saturday dawned a blustery, cold, windy day, she felt noticeably calm. Out in the field, Rachelle and JaNae had been working on the combine together until JaNae jumped down and ran to the end of the field for goggles to protect her eyes. Clint was running a windrower a little ahead of the combine.

As the combine reached the end of the potato row, the driver got out to talk to the boss who had just arrived. Rachelle, in her naturally industrious way, climbed down off the combine, crowbar in hand, and knelt down in front of the wheel to clean the rock bucket. The rest of the kids had remained on top of the equipment, and when the driver started up the tractor, he didn't see Rachelle nor could he hear the cries to stop. As he pulled forward, the wheel caught Rachelle's legs and rolled up her body, crushing her with enormous weight.

Realizing that his sister was badly hurt, Clint

jumped in the pickup and went for his parents. The wind was blowing terribly, but as Stuart and Joan reached the scene, even the weather was peaceful and calm. The Spirit already attended them as they drove. The same spiritual comfort would attend Joan for the next several months.

The EMT's had already been called, and as Stuart and the boss prepared to bless Rachelle, he knew in his heart that she was gone. After the anointing, he could only say, "We love you, Rachelle. Heavenly Father loves you, and He will take good care of you." Heartbroken sobs filled the air as friends and family huddled in sorrow at the tragic loss of such a beautiful daughter. Rachelle had stepped through the veil, and she had spent her last week in this mortal existence. Her eyes were now open clearly, and as they were, her father was allowed a momentary glimpse into eternity.

"There were two impressions I received," Stuart testified. "It was just like a flash in my mind. In the first one, I saw Rachelle lying on the ground and a figure in white was lifting her from her body assisting her to her feet. The next one came when we were in the hospital. In my mind I saw Rachelle being introduced to several people. She had the same bashful smile on her face that she used to have in similar circumstances. I had the distinct impression that one of the men was Joan's grandfather. There were four or five other people around that I didn't recognize as this flashed in my mind. I can still remember that smile on her face, but the picture left me and never came back."

"Peace I Leave with You"

The Hall family and the entire community grieved at such a loss, especially sorrowful for those involved in the accident. In love and compassion, Stuart and Joan visited the homes of all who had witnessed the trauma and especially reached out in love to the man who had been driving the combine, a dear friend who truly loved Rachelle also. They both expressed that "We could never have any bad feelings, or add to his pain. It was an accident. We just couldn't be bitter." Joan admits to being an emotional person and says, "I have relived that scene a thousand times in my mind. Once I considered what it would have been like if I had reacted in shock and behaved out of control. The pain I felt as I imagined that scene was twice as bad. I'm so thankful the Lord's spirit was with me right from the beginning—strengthening me. I'm so grateful that I didn't do or say anything that would hurt anyone or make me feel guilty the rest of my life. My heart hurts so much worse to think of myself out of control."

Rachelle surely looked upon her mother that day with love and approval as she witnessed her strength. Joan readily admits that she couldn't have handled the situation if it hadn't been for previous promptings the Spirit had blessed her with. "I knew that someone from our family was needed on the other side to do an important work. None of my mother's family are members of the Church. I know as soon as I get going on genealogy, Rachelle and I will work hand in hand." Joan was called to work at the extraction center in Pocatello shortly after the accident, and at the time of this writing is an assistant coordinator.

Stuart described the most difficult part as waking up in the morning with a cold feeling, realizing that Rachelle's death was a reality and not a bad dream. He is a gifted artist and has insight that is highly developed. Perhaps it is the sensitivity and the training of the artist's eye that allows him to create visually what he spiritually sees. His great ability can be felt throughout this work in his beautiful sketches.

The scene that flashed through his mind at the accident kept recurring over and over. He had had a very difficult time dealing with the agony and pain his daughter must have felt as the wheel climbed her legs and ran up her body. The most comforting thing he had to cling to is a scripture shared by an understanding bishop at the viewing: "And it shall come to pass that those that die in me shall not taste of death, for it shall be sweet unto them." (D&C 42:46)

"Then one day on the bus to work, the picture came into my mind again. It finally dawned on me. It was like a light bulb lit up in my mind. When the figure in white was lifting Rachelle up, the wheel was still behind her. It was at her feet. I don't think that she really had to feel pain. I think she was spared that. I've read many after-life stories, and in all the experiences related, they never talk about the pain. As I visited with the kids who had been on the combine that day, they all said that as the combine started up her feet, she just laid over like she was asleep. What a comfort to know that my impression was right and true."

All the beautiful and fine things that Rachelle represented, she took with her into eternity. She sees clearly now, as tears and clouds of despair sometimes block our view. Her vision is clear. These are the things she would say to us, as expressed by her Uncle Roger at her services:

"Weep for me today, but tomorrow smile and think of all the fun we've shared—the night slumber parties, the talks, the laughs, the good things like track and volleyball. Remember the good things. Grow close together. Friendship is a sacred thing; it never dies. Be strong and do what's right. I want my family to know I love them, that they are my best friends."

The day after Thanksgiving, 1987, the Hall family, along with Joan's family, met at the Idaho Falls Temple. Joan took Rachelle's name through the temple for her ordinances and endowment, and Grandpa Herb and Grandma Dona were sealed to their five children after forty-two years of marriage. Rachelle's life and passing had united her family. As they clasped hands and knelt across the altar that day, not only was it witnessed by angels, but also by Rachelle's deep understanding eyes and radiant smile.

"My Sister, My Friend"

She always seemed to be there
When days were dark and blue,
She'd always be there waiting
To talk to after school.

She always seemed so perfect,
She always seemed so good,
We didn't want to let her go
But we did what we knew we should.

She always had a smile
And something good to say,
For if we live the word of God
We'll see her again someday.

She always seemed so happy
She always seemed to care,
For what she knew inside herself
That it was love she had to share.

This girl is my sister,
This girl is my friend.
He took her just to borrow,
We gave her just to lend.

JaNae Hall
1987

CHAPTER SIX

Taking Charge of Life

Ruth

To catch a moonbeam,
To clutch the wind,
To fly to the moon without a rocket
Are ordinary next to you, my friend.

Success in life isn't what you get out of it but what you become by it; is a statement not merely spoken, but daily lived by Ruth Gneiting.

Her words of counsel have brought inspiration into the lives of both young and old, and her life serves as a beacon to help each passer-by survive the tumult of mortality.

To imply that Ruth is an ordinary woman would be like implying the Hoover Dam could be restrained by a picket fence. She is as comfortable and at ease straddling a horse helping with cattle at roundup as she would be sitting in the state legislature.

Politics have always held an interest for Ruth. Issues affecting the future of her state and especially proposals of moral judgment always aroused her concern. She was particularly a "fighter" when it came to the passage of laws that she strongly felt were detrimental to human rights. One such issue was the Equal Rights Amendment. She certainly felt compassion for women and their needs; nevertheless, she recognized the bill before the legislature at that time would not provide for the needs of women, but would, in fact, take some of their freedoms away.

Most of the states had ratified the bill, and her home state of Idaho was no exception. However, she felt very strongly there was a better way. As the time came nearer for the vote to be cast for this issue, Ruth, along with a busload of other women and a few husbands, traveled to Boise, the state capital, to meet with the legislature. The lines were clearly and firmly drawn. One senator held the deciding vote. He had the reputation of being fair and willing to listen to his constituents, and Ruth had faith in the old adage, "If there is a will, there is definitely a way." The moment came. The dignitary who held so much in his hands entered the room. He had undoubtedly expected a group of hostile and somewhat fanatical women, but Ruth had made certain this would not be the case.

Prior to his arrival, she counseled with the

assembly and explained the importance of not being angry or contentious. She instructed them in proper conduct and the respect that should be shown to this man and his office as a leader of their state.

As the dignitary entered the room, proper protocol took place as the entire assembly of men and women stood and thunderous applause filled the hall.

He raised his hand in silence, as he shook his head in immediate disbelief . . . "Who is the spokesman for this group?" the senator asked, half smiling.

"I am, Senator!" came a pleasant reply from the back of the room, as the charismatic and smiling "Ruthie" enthusiastically walked down the aisle to meet her guest. A tailored suit of softest pastel and a gently ruffled blouse, her trademark of femininity, enhanced dark shining eyes and silver-grey hair. And yet, an inward beauty and radiance far beyond physical appearance was immediately recognized. As every eye followed her to center stage, anticipation filled the air. Ruth was indeed in charge!

She politely and persuasively presented the views of the group and asked for the senator's support. Before the entire assembly, she stood with dignity and expressed her beliefs with strength and conviction. The truth spoken by this dignified and knowledgeable daughter of God touched the Senator's heart and made final determination in his vote. The bill was rescinded!

Ruth became a candidate for the state legislature in 1982 and her campaign was looking very promising. She and her husband, Keith, made the decision the last of April, and this decision turned her life into a rigorous upheaval. But Ruth had some very strong convictions about her state and how certain things should be done, and she wanted to have a hand in making it happen.

The following months were filled with excitement. Organizing a good campaign committee full of enthusiasm for her success was first on the docket. Then, of course, her "homework" had to be done; and she would be ready with an answer for any question which would come her way. There were meetings to be organized, personal visits to make, and articles to write. Her views needed to be heard, so the best source of advertising had to be considered and then carefully planned and executed.

Volunteers to help Ruth in her political adventures came in all sizes and ages. Grade school, high school, and college students, family and friends took a seat on the Gneiting bandwagon. "It was an exhilarating and delightful time. It was both rewarding and sobering and filled with learning experiences and interesting people," recalled the vivacious Ruth.

It was the best of times and the worst of times.

Time passed quickly and almost too soon it was October 24; nine more days and the campaigning and the election would be over. Ruth had been burning the candle at both ends while campaigning for state representative and taking care of things on the "home front." October also meant "roundup" time as late fall weather and threatening winter storms in the high country signalled to ranchers the annual hauling of cattle down from summer ranges was at hand. Ruth loved the outdoors and all her married life had helped with the family farming and ranching operation. Levis, boots, and a bandana transformed this "elegant lady" into a top-notch cowhand who could handle a horse, throw a lariat, or brand a calf along with the best of them. Over the years, she had become a priceless and pretty asset as neighbors, young and old, gathered to round up their herds for winter. Ruth was well known for her bottomless lunches that could feed the entire crew and half the state of Idaho or anyone else that showed up; hungry and tired riders knew there was "always plenty" if they rode with Ruth. Many days required over fourteen hours in the saddle, but regardless of how long and dusty the ride or blustery the weather, Ruth would always arrive at trail's end with the hardiest of men.

Being unable to help much this year had been the candidate's biggest sacrifice. So this October 24, even though she had been out campaigning late the night before, Ruth insisted she could go into the hills and at least drive a truckload of cattle out. At 4:30 a.m. she left for Bone, Idaho, in a cattle truck to pick up the first load of calves. A second truck would come later, driven by Gneiting's oldest son, Jay.

"While they loaded my truck, I fixed breakfast in the little camp house for Keith and our son, Danny, and a friend. I enjoyed having a few minutes to fuss over them. The campaign had been so busy and involved that I hadn't had much time to spend with my family, and I really missed that closeness. As I watched them work that morning, I could only contemplate how lucky I was and felt so grateful to have all of them. Life was exciting, and I truly had the best of both worlds!"

When the men finished loading her truck, Ruth headed home. Her mind returned to the campaign, and she was absorbed in mentally debating political issues. The following week she and her opponent were scheduled for a television "phone-in" question-and-answer program. As she drove, her mind was completely inundated with plans for every day until the election.

Within a matter of seconds, Ruth's world would be turned upside down (as well as her truck). Little did she realize that tragedy and a literal transformation of her daily life lay directly ahead, for she would never be quite the same again. Both she and her family would be called on to draw on resources they never knew they possessed. An unknown inner strength would enter their lives to feed their souls, bandage their hearts, and give them courage to face another day.

Hauling cattle was not a new venture to the experienced driver, so her loved ones thought she apparently had fallen asleep that morning while coming down a steep hill, and then awoke as her truck and twenty-foot trailer carrying twenty-one calves and a cow approached a dangerous and unmarked S-curve in the road.

Ruth remembered carefully applying the brakes,

but she failed to negotiate the curve with the heavy load and the truck began to roll.

"When I realized what was happening, I thought, 'Oh, dear, I'm wrecking our truck'!" In seconds, the truck and the cattle rack were completely demolished and left lying in shambles, with only piles of wood remaining as the load heaved one-and-a-half times down the embankment.

Miraculously, only one calf had to be destroyed, and although two strayed, the others were left unhurt but assuredly dazed. The same, unfortunately, was not the lot of the driver. Ruth suffered a broken back, a damaged liver covered with dangerous blood blisters, a bruised heart, collapsed lung, broken ribs, and a scalping job that even a Navajo warrior would have been impressed with. It seemed impossible to even hope there would not be brain damage. "I had never imagined an accident like this could ever happen to me! But it did! And it can happen to anyone," exclaimed Ruth.

As the wreckage thundered to a stop on the hillside, Ruth slipped in and out of consciousness with confused thoughts of "Whose foot is on my chest?" Fear clutched her as she strained to remember where Keith was. Reassurance came, as she sorted out in her mind that he was in the other truck and miles ahead. When consciousness sporadically returned, her thoughts were always centered on someone else. "I'm so glad I didn't bring my grandchildren," her mind whispered in relief. "It's my foot that's crushing my chest!" she realized.

For the unbearable to become bearable, the Lord provides the safety valve of unconsciousness. It took one and one-half hours for an emergency team to cut Ruth free from the wreckage, and paramedics worked another hour at the scene attempting to stabilize her for transport. She was then immediately taken to the nearest hospital in Idaho Falls, only to find a neurosurgeon was not immediately available. With her life hanging in the balance, the ambulance rushed her on to Pocatello.

Anxious and frightened family members stood numbly outside the trauma unit awaiting the doctor's decision on surgery. What now? What will it take to repair the damage? Will she walk again? He paused, looking into worried and tear-streaked faces, and then spoke deafening words, "I don't know. The first thing I have to do is save her life."

But Ruth's mind had never considered dying or giving up as one of the options. The accident that left her more dead than alive occurred on Sunday, and miraculously on Wednesday, prayers and fasting and sheer determination on Ruth's part, enabled her to undergo back surgery to have her spine fused and two herringbone rods implanted.

Keith, her husband and faithful companion of thirty-five years, slept on the floor, in the waiting room, while she was listed as extremely critical in the intensive care unit. "His prayers kept me alive for the first few days, so he's stuck with me now," Ruth said with a smile. But Keith is more than pleased to be stuck. When doctors told him that Ruth was paralyzed, his first thought was, "Thank God, she is alive."

Blessings were administered, ward and stake fasts were held, and prayers ascended to the heavens by the hundreds. Ruth is the first to say that those prayers were heard and answered, although maybe not as they had hoped, that she would soon be well and back to her active self. After weeks of suffering, the medical world's final word to her was, "You will be in a wheelchair for the rest of your life."

After this heartbreaking pronouncement, Ruth found herself daily and many times hourly repeating to herself the AA's Serenity Prayer. "God grant me the serenity to accept the things I cannot change, and the courage to change the things I can: and the wisdom to know the difference." And to this prayer she added a personal plea. "But God, give me the courage not to give up on what I think is right, even though I may think it is hopeless."

During the four months she was in the hospital, her sense of humor was very evident as she described her experience in the stryker frame. "I was placed on the frame, laying on my back and they laid another one over me, bolted me from top to bottom. I looked just like an Oreo cookie! There were three straps to hold me in place and levers on each end which the nurses used to turn me. Every two hours they would come into my room and count one, two, three, and together flip me over."

Ruth was an example to patients and staff alike as she underwent excruciating pain which accompanied the rehabilitation. During one of her sessions in rehab she was working between the parallel bars when she felt a burning sensation in her leg. It was diagnosed as deepvein thrombosis caused by months of immobility. The blood flow has a tendency to become sluggish and the area drained by the vein became swollen and extremely painful as the normal flow of blood was obstructed. Her leg was swollen to the size of three. There were also complications from the internal injuries, as well as lack of movement. At one time her digestive system did not function for nineteen days, which added greatly to her misery.

Through it all she remained strong and didn't allow herself to dwell on any hatred or bitterness. Her attitude remained, "I wish it hadn't happened—but it did. It is just another of the many interruptions that come into our lives, and it was probably due to my own carelessness."

There were some bad days, but it was important to Ruth to keep strong for the family as they visited and stayed close by her side. She did not want the other patients to see her cry, so she confined her sadness until late in the evenings when tears were shed alone.

Unanswered questions came to her in the still darkness of the night. "Did I agree to this before I came?" It was Sunday, but the "ox was in the mire." The Lord did not cause this accident; she could always reassure herself of that. And why not? Through each of her daily trials she could feel His presence and the sweet peace which only He can give. Assurance came as the Spirit whispered to her soul, "The Lord thy God shall lead thee by the hand, and give thee answers to thy prayers." (D&C 112:10) Ruth had put her hand in the Lord's.

February 17, 1983, dawned a red-letter day; after four months Ruth was being released from the hospital. However, the homecoming would be another great adjustment. Even Ruth, who was proficient in meeting challenges, found herself unprepared for the exertion it would take to reach self-reliance. More than anything she wanted to emerge from this experience independent. Dependence on others was intrinsic to her nature. Excellent care and motivation from the doctors and nursing staff helped prepare her mentally to meet this interruption.

Inwardly Ruth was struggling to come to grips with the situation. She had already faced tremendous disappointment and crushed dreams in being unable to actively complete the campaign. Although she and her active life were temporarily slowed down, in her heart she knew that it was not the "end of the world."

For nine months, Ruth was confined to a body cast called a "turtle shell." Gone were the soft pastels and tailored suits. T-shirts became her only wardrobe, and the highlight of each day was an evening back rub.

"What a thrill when it was finally removed, and I could bend over my chair and pick something up off the floor!"

"Keith was literally my 'around-the-clock' nurse and, he did everything for me, and I do mean everything."

In spite of the encouragement she received from counseling and in therapy, she still experienced low days and many frustrations. "What I used to accomplish in twenty minutes now takes me an hour to do," she sighed.

She learned to sweep the floor by brushing the broom and dirt toward her so she could bend to scoop it up. "Imagine cleaning a broken egg up off the floor from a wheelchair. It can be done," Ruth said very positively. "Even though it is one of those tasks that frustrates even those not hindered by the chair. Don't believe everything you see in the movies, either," she said laughing, "operating a wheelchair isn't as easy as it looks."

She quickly learned persistence was the key in turning any difficult problem into a much smaller one. And persistence did pay off for Ruth as she eventually learned to compensate for the loss of her legs. She worked diligently in the rehab unit to strengthen her arms which became a great asset to her future.

The only compensation made for her disability is Ruth's wheelchair ramp by the door. Nothing else in her home has been altered.

For five out of the seven years since Ruth's accident, the women of the Lakeview Ward Relief Society came to her home to give her "range of motion" therapy. This devotion from her sisters in the gospel would pay many other dividends in her life.

Most of the feeling is back in her legs, although they are numb to the touch. She also has some movement in both legs. She is proud to show her capability as she shakes her legs as evidence. She can take her right foot off the foot rest of the chair and kick with it but is presently unable to move her left leg, without the aid of her hands. "Even though I still can't walk, I have come a long way because of the sisters in Relief Society and their diligence in coming every day and giving me therapy."

Nearly a full year after the accident Ruth entered the Elks Rehabilitation Center in Boise, Idaho. The first day of treatment she fell and tore ligaments in her leg, and the injury also caused painful blood clots. In spite of her new injuries, Ruth's constant smile and cheerful attitude concealed to others her intense suffering.

"I count my blessings every day for the use of my arms because I met so many friends while in Boise who can't use theirs," remarked Ruth. "They are people, just like you and me, whose lives have been tragically interrupted, many times in the prime of life. People need to be aware of the problems the disabled face daily. You never know when it will happen and to whom."

Strong faith in God has been Ruth's mainstay during dark and difficult times. She knows it is a medical miracle to have so much movement and feeling in her legs.

"I still believe in miracles, and if the Lord is willing, I'll walk again. If not, He must have other plans for me that I can do from the chair. To walk again may not come in this life—but when it does, I will be ready."

For a cattleman, there is always work that has to be done around the ranch. Ruth had always been

Keith's right-hand man, and she missed riding her horse almost more than walking itself. The task of earning a living was a definite concern, and Ruth desperately missed being a part of things. In spite of her handicap she longed to participate and to be involved again, and especially she desired to be a help to her companion.

She reminded herself many times, "Where there's a will . . ." and then she would take a long hard look at what needed to be done and begin working at a solution. She decided to learn to use an extended arm (wire prongs) to get things from her cabinets and put dishes away; and she discovered she could do her work sideways from her chair. Soon she mastered cooking from the side of the stove. Although she could no longer go outside to help Keith with the cattle, she resolved she could at least have his meals prepared and pack the much-needed lunches. Little by little, she began to feel more productive.

Shortly before Christmas in December of 1987, Keith and Ruth were up at 4 a.m. preparing to take a trip to Montana for a cattle sale. Everything was packed and ready to go. Ruth had finished last minute details and in the wintry darkness hurried down the ramp to go to the car. Suddenly the wheelchair slipped off the edge and threw Ruth onto her knees. She heard her legs snap as she landed and both of them were seriously fractured. "I know the accident would have done much more damage if my legs had not been so limber from the treatments given to me by the women in Relief Society," commented Ruth.

Once again misfortune did not stop Ruth. She was in the hospital for only a brief stay and even though she was experiencing excruciating pain, she returned home and resumed her household chores. Only a few changes were made in her daily routine. She said, "My legs stuck straight out in front of me, so I cleared out a space on the third shelf of the refrigerator. That way I could roll myself right inside when I needed to get food out to prepare meals. It worked pretty slick and really didn't slow me down too much."

Very little slows Ruth down today. After she had her car equipped with hand controls, she traveled to Boise for the required driver's training program. Once again diligence and hard work paid off. Learning to drive with hand controls was the first step leading to her independence in the outside world. Next came putting her chair in the back seat and removing it. Persistence conquered the tremendous challenge and "Ruthie" makes the difficult task of being completely self-reliant look easy.

Her only daughter, Vickie, is devoted to her mother and has always seen to her wants and transportation needs. But now Ruth takes great pride and satisfaction as she is able to come and go and carry on with life. Now she frequently "picks up" Vickie for a day's outing. To maintain her independence in any situation, whether help is available or not, Ruth slides to the passenger side of the car, removes her chair from the back seat, and places it alongside of the car seat. She next places a slick board underneath her and partially in the chair. After sliding into the chair, she replaces the left arm rest, and double-checks the safety of her chair, and then she's on her way.

As an active member of the LDS church, Ruth feels visiting teaching is a must as well as attending all her church meetings. She is also diligent in filling her assignment at the data processing center. This necessitates an eighty-mile round trip from Sterling to Pocatello once a week. Many times she drives alone, even during winter months. Her devotion to the gospel of Jesus Christ and her enduring belief in its principles and teachings have been a constant guide in everything she does. The same Spirit which kept her going on dark days now gives her the energy to reach out to others in need, for she said, "It is so important we never look down on anyone. And equally important that we always recognize our own self-worth." Reaching out is second nature to Ruth. In spite of her own problems, she is a remarkable person with a tremendous attitude and zest for life. There is no place in Ruth's life for hate or bitterness, but unlimited room for humor and loving encouragement to others.

Much of Ruth's time is spent in service to others. Fully active in the Republican Party, she has lobbied for such issues as Right to Work and Right to Life. She serves on committees to help increase public awareness of the tremendous need for accessibility for the handicapped, reminding others, "Remember, it can happen to anyone."

Ruth is well known as a gifted teacher and is continually sought after as a speaker. Her life and insight and testimony of a loving Father, have lifted men and women—young and old, married and single—throughout the area where she lives. Faith and courage have been restored to many as Ruthie visits various organizations and offers love and understanding. The Lord has indeed a great work for His beloved daughter to perform from her chair. But when you see Ruth, you won't see the chair. Instead of a disability, she has a great ability, to live life to its fullest and inspire others to meet obstacles and make the best of their situations.

Ruth feels, "Whenever God closes a door, He opens a window. And the sun does shine again! I have learned that we can either take charge and rule our lives, or we can give up and dwell in self pity and useless frustration."

A local news article described Ruth Gneiting as "Sterling's Ray of Sunshine" and the phrase is readily agreed upon by all who meet her. To know her or of her is one of life's greatest blessings. She radiates beauty wherever she goes and none see in her a handicap but only her "wholeness of body and spirit." As Ruth smilingly says, "I haven't stopped, I've just slowed down a little."

She has no time for asking "Why?" but instead the enthusiasm and courage to say "Why not?"

She testifies, "We know God is in control of our interruptions, disabilities, successes, and handicaps. He knows our capacity perfectly, and He placed us here to succeed! Whenever or whatever the Lord needs of me, I will be ready."

CHAPTER SEVEN

An Everlasting Bond

Sam and Kathy

"Trust in the Lord with all thine heart; and lean not unto thine own understanding" (Prov. 3:5)

His voice sounded just as she had imagined it would as he quietly said, "Kathy, would you like to have dinner with me tonight?" Thinking she was alone in the office, the sound of his voice startled her, and she bumped her knee as she quickly rose from the file cabinet. Any tell-tale pain was soon forgotten as she looked into the face of the young, shy and handsome truck driver, Sam. She had noticed him ever since she began to work for the grocery company and had hoped he might take an interest in her, and now he had. Caught so off-guard, her answer was a somewhat startled and weak, though definitely pleased, "Yes."

That first date was everything Kathy had hoped as Sam took her hand and very soon her heart. Across the table in the restaurant dining room, the atmosphere was warm and comfortably relaxed. The dark-eyed beauty mused to herself how upset her parents would be to witness the scene. She knew from "talk" in the office that Sam had just gone through a divorce, and strict Nazarene parents would definitely not approve of their nineteen-year-old daughter seeing a divorced man.

"Here I am," she thought, "my first time on my own and away from home and literally throwing caution to the wind!"

Who was this kind and sensitive Sam that made her feel so royal? His tall, lean exterior revealed bright, shining teeth, blue eyes, and wavy hair but something quite beyond physical handsomeness intrigued Kathy. She observed large, strong and calloused hands, a sure sign of hard work, yet well-groomed and adept at social skills. Little could she know of the labor, experiences, and life they signified. Sam bore the hands of his father, a kind and gentle man who cared for his wife's every need when debilitating arthritis in later life left her an invalid. This strong yet gentle man raised Sam and his younger brothers and sisters in the quiet, though sometimes harsh, beauty of Bear Lake County, Idaho.

There the Matthews family knew first hand the temporal and emotional ravage of the Great Depression of the Thirties. Bleak years brought no markets for the family's sheep, and when winter feed became nonexistent, several bands had to be destroyed to prevent their slow starvation. Without the proceeds from a small herd of cows milked by hand, the family would have been destitute. Young Sam witnessed the seemingly senseless waste and heartaches. Literally hundreds of sheep were gone. At least in retrospect, that didn't seem as bad as had the long and endless days when he tended them in the hills. Many nights he would stay to keep watch under the stars, and then at sunrise begin the six-mile trip home on his horse to get ready for a day's study in the little two-room schoolhouse. Although it was far from being his favorite activity, Sam realized "it had to be done." And even sheepherding had its compensations, for Sam became an excellent hunter and expert fisherman.

Having good friends, participating in youth government, and being selected basketball team captain were highlights of Sam's teenage years at Fielding High School. A call to the Central States Mission was Sam's first look at the outside world. The necessary sixty dollars a month was a continued support and willing sacrifice of a loving family. When he returned home, America was at undeclared war with Korea. Having the same willingness to serve his country as his Father in Heaven, Sam enlisted.

Halfway around the world, Sam found himself the only Mormon in his regiment and seemingly in the whole, strange land. He searched out others of his faith and, with fifteen or twenty other servicemen, held the first LDS service in Korea. Many times he "took a stand" for his beliefs and withstood animosity and criticism. He cheerfully took a lot of ribbing and proudly became known as "the Mormon."

Now here tonight for the first time a new light had come into his life as he was warmed by the glow of this black-eyed, radiant beauty. Basque and Hungarian she had confided were part of her ancestry, although as a child her nationality had been ofttimes mistaken. Her thick black hair and delicate skin glistened in the candle's glow.

She too was from a rural Idaho community, the firstborn of devout members of a Nazarene church. At one time her father became a minister, and his first clergy assignment took the family to South Dakota. The meager salary could not provide for Kathy and her younger brothers and sisters, so the family returned to Idaho. Although the Gaceys were strict disciplinarians, love for their children was always evident. They loved the Lord and always worshipped as a family in Sunday church services.

In the second grade, little dark-eyed Kathy encountered the challenge to stand true to beliefs she held sacred. On this particular day, the teacher had taught the children the lyrics and dance to the "Hokey Pokey." It looked like a lot of fun and Kathy ached to join in, but the teachings of her parents were uppermost in her mind, and she explained to the teacher that her religion forbade her to participate. From the side she watched, feeling very much alone, and in her young mind wondered, "How come?"

One year Kathy's academic instruction came

from a Nazarene parochial school. She recognized the altruistic behavior of her parents and ministers, and yet their teachings seemed confusing. At revival meetings, the congregation would be encouraged to come forward, confess their need for repentance, and then be saved. Her mind visualized a frightening and punishing God. Many times she was afraid to leave the meeting and feared condemnation because she had not gone to the altar.

"I loved my parents, and I knew they believed what they taught me and what the ministers said. But I just couldn't participate regardless of how frightened I was or how much I loved them. I kept thinking, 'If this is right, I shouldn't be so frightened.'" She somehow believed in a "loving God," although she knew Him not.

Ambitious and responsible, Kathy held a part-time job all through school. Following graduation from Borah High, she moved to Pocatello to live with her Aunt Doris, who was also a close friend. She was excited to be on her own, and the secretarial position she had just landed at Associated Foods would bring much more than she expected.

The beautiful, dark-haired girl from an entirely different background gave some meaning once again to Sam's life. They became a twosome, and after a few dates he told her of his beliefs and of his desire for her to learn more about his religion. But she wasn't interested. It wasn't long until Sam declared his love and asked for Kathy's hand. The proposal was accompanied with "I love you, but I cannot marry someone not of my faith." Kathy decided if it were that important to Sam, she would take the missionary lessons. After two discussions, she announced she was "marrying a man, not a religion."

"I'm sure I knew it was true even then," she recalled, "but deep within lay the teachings of my parents, and I knew how badly it would hurt them. And I loved them so."

The Gaceys were understandably hurt and disappointed that Kathy chose to marry out of her faith. A heartbroken father even threatened to disown her if she married a "Mormon," but his love surpassed his pain, and he eventually accepted Sam as a son.

Joined Hands

Following the wedding, Sam continued to encourage his bride to take additional missionary lessons. After the second series, she still answered with an emphatic, "no." Three years later, while expecting her first child, she consented to listen again. As the young missionaries began, she confided, "I don't want to waste your time. I know the Book of Mormon is true, and the Church is true, but it's Joseph Smith I can't accept." Without hesitation one young missionary bore testimony that without Joseph Smith there would be no church. Feeling the Spirit bear witness of truth, Kathy extended her hand in a faith that required the bending of her whole soul and probable disassociation with loved ones and asked for baptism.

This mighty and great change that entered her heart would alter and interrupt life as she knew it. Conversion would take her from bittersweet choice to strength and conviction to withstand great trials and adversity. After the "trial of faith," the witness is given. Kathy had met this trial of faith, and she would see countless blessings come forth in witness.

A desire to return to the land remained with Sam over the years. He and Kathy's lives had been blessed with two little girls, and he wanted them to grow up where they could run and be free. One day he spotted a place for them—a small farm of one hundred acres, west across the reservoir in Pingree. The only home was a "shack," and the land needed developing. Still, it seemed the perfect place to build their dreams.

Today, the girls share fond memories of summer in the shack, but for Sam and Kathy who both continued to travel the sixty-mile round trip to work on separate schedules, the vision was much more realistic. There was no phone, and water had to be heated on a potbelly stove; the walls were paper thin, and the roof leaked. It was anything but a dream, but they were building a life together. Summer days filled little one's hands with clusters of wild flowers or a "chance" to pick rocks for a penny a piece (to buy a trampoline) or tenderly caring for baby farm animals.

Eventually, Sam and Kathy moved a trailer in, requiring Kathy to give up her beautiful home in town, and the Matthews became year-round residents of Pingree. In spite of the hardships, they loved their new life. People were kind and good to them, and Kathy thought she was truly in heaven as life unfolded and she grew in the gospel. Another child was on the way, and she would soon be blessed again with the gift of life. She could hardly fathom that the Lord would trust her so fully as to allow her participation in His ultimate creation.

The young couple had already formed a partnership with God and in the spring of 1976 felt a strong desire to have the bond sealed forever. Eager and fully prepared to come unto the Lord's altar, Kathy's heart nearly burst with joy as she and Sam and their three beautiful daughters, all clothed in spotless white, kneeled in God's holy temple. With clasped hands over a sacred altar, they were sealed for eternity in a bond that would never die.

The little family grew spiritually and physically. The tiny trailer began to burst at the seams. Another six years had brought the birth of two more beautiful girls.

Building a home "from scratch"—an awesome task for most, became the Matthews' next exciting adventure. New skills were developed and willing hands united by this dream. At last the endless sanding and ominous challenge of painting to the top of vaulted ceilings were finished. Not even four-foot snowdrifts could dampen spirits as the family moved in just before Christmas. Who said it couldn't be done? It and everything Kathy tackled was overcome—that is, almost everything.

A woman's most dreaded fear became a reality as one day Kathy noticed a strange and abnormal lump. A prompt visit to the doctor assured her it was nothing dangerous but only fibrocystic disease. A two-year, regular follow-up program continued until Kathy sensed something was very wrong. A visit to a surgeon validated her concern. The prognosis was cancer.

Her mind raced wildly. How? Why? She had faithfully and trustingly kept close and precautionary exam dates, but somehow the cancer had remained hidden, yet steadily growing, deep within breast tissue. Surgery was immediately scheduled but not performed until after a priesthood blessing. As hands were placed on her head, a warm and comforting assurance spread through Kathy's soul, and she knew everything would be okay. Adversity caused her to turn to God as she had never done before in her life. She prayed for help and assurance that He was there. She had taken her Book of Mormon to the hospital with her and every day, besides the many hours she spent reading when she needed a special lift, she would open the scriptures with a prayer in her heart, lay her hand on the page and read. Without exception what she read would seem just for her, and comfort came.

Her recovery was swift though not painless. She refused to be defeated and insisted that returning quickly to work (rural mail delivery) would be the best therapy for her temporarily impaired right arm. Quickly accepting her loss, she was fitted for prosthesis. Kathy had witnessed the ravages of this cruel disease in her father's life. Before its threat personally encompassed her, she had firmly resolved that under no conditions would she submit to the nightmare of chemotherapy.

But now with her own life on the line, she confided to a friend, "When you personally face it, you no longer consider what it will physically do to you—but what it could mean to your children. Even if it only 'buys' you another year or two in time, to teach and prepare your little ones, it is worth it."

The chemo, with its unpleasant side effects ranging from headaches to severe hemorrhaging that plagued Kathy constantly, was rarely discussed or acknowledged. And it seemed to "buy" more than just time. Life developed a new dimension as Kathy enjoyed simple things she had never noticed before, and each day took on new meaning.

Unpleasant months finally passed, and the radiant glow returned to Kathy's face. This painful and unwanted interruption had brought new understanding and appreciation for life.

Four Years Later

The schedule remained busy and hectic at home as Sam juggled a truck-driving career with part-time farming. His long-distance trucking route required him to leave home somewhere between twelve midnight and 3 a.m. to make 6 a.m. grocery deliveries. A citation for twenty-five years of driving accident-free and his work record showing he had never missed a single day for illness in over thirty years demonstrated he was not only capable but also highly dependable.

Suddenly Sam lost twenty pounds without

apparent reason. He also experienced a strange difficulty in swallowing, and many times he had to pull his rig to the side of the road so he could get out and stand to swallow. At first he tried altering his diet, but soon even liquids caused difficulty.

Fear struck the Matthews' home again as Sam read of malignant symptoms. The doctor's tests confirmed the suspicion—cancer of the esophagus. "Oh, surely, Dear Lord, not Sam," Kathy cried from the depths of her soul. It had only been four short years since her surgery, and they were just getting a little normalcy to their lives. How could this be happening again?

As Sam began to understand his life-and-death situation, he learned that cells from the lining of his esophagus had, for an unknown reason, quickly multiplied and formed a tumor that grew until it constricted the passageway to his stomach. Usually this disorder was linked to irritants like tobacco smoke or alcohol. Sam was not indulging in either, and logic offered no understanding.

They had bravely faced the last great trauma, but how could they face this? What had happened to life? The analogy of the "Gardner and the Currant Bush" became painfully real. Just when life at last seemed full, when testimonies had blossomed and spirits were growing in stature, it seemed as though the Lord was pruning and cutting back to the very quick of the soul. Painfully the wounds wept and tearfilled nights questioned why a loving Gardner would allow such pain. But, as He promised long ago,

He remained at their side as grief and suffering and searching tapped an inner strength that sent forth deep roots of strong, unwavering spiritual growth. They would accept the situation and hold unfaltering trust in the Gardner's hand.

Without treatment Sam's chances for survival were zero. A "patch-up" job locally would offer only a 10% hope. The family was stunned by the prognosis. Sam's only chance was in a specialized surgery performed only in Omaha, Nebraska, by a Dr. DeMeester. The long and anxious waiting game began.

Word finally came. Sam's case had been accepted. How would the family's finances and mundane routines be met? And what of the children left wondering and bewildered at home?

So many questions and uncertainties had to be swiftly resolved as life became an emotional roller coaster.

The two older girls had become beautiful young women, and an aunt and uncle scheduled vacation time to help them care for the children.

Family, friends, and the entire community were humbled by cancer's atrocious second attack in the Matthews' home. Everyone sought to help, and one friend contacted Church leaders in the Omaha area seeking aid for Sam and Kathy when they arrived alone and unsettled, strangers in their city. The Relief Society president to whom she spoke on the phone answered simply, and unhesitatingly, "We will take up where you people in Idaho leave off." True to her word, when the plane landed in Omaha, she and the visiting teaching leader met them at the airport and familiarized them with St. Joseph's Hospital. Through the ordeal, Kathy stayed with the stake Relief Society president and her husband, who generously supplied her with transportation to and from the hospital.

The Testing Begins

Intricate tests were required on every part of Sam's body to determine if he would qualify for the extensive surgery procedure. Heart and lungs were analyzed, and a colonostopy was ordered to determine if his organs were healthy and the blood supply adequate. An angiogram inserted through the groin analyzed the aorta, and finally a video scope of the stomach and duodenum completed the inspection. As Sam remarked, "I checked my pride in at the front desk."

Decision

Dr. DeMeester determined Sam was a good candidate for surgery and informed the anxious couple of the probable statistics. If the cancer had not left the lining of the esophagus and no other glands were affected, Sam's chance of survival was 98%; if it were in one or the other, 60%. If it had done both, recovery was a slim 18%. But without treatment, Sam's chances were nil.

Relief and fear simultaneously tugged at anxious hearts, but by the appointed surgery hour,

Sam was confident in his doctor as well as in the outcome.

Memories were vivid of the ward fast and the priesthood blessings given to him and Kathy by the stake president. Friends and loved ones gathered in faith and supplication for the Lord's blessing as they had met together the Sunday before their departure. Sam knew well that the "fervent prayer of the righteous availeth much," and he felt of the strength as they rolled him away. At home, anxious and stricken daughters waited by the phone.

Kathy knew it would take nearly thirteen hours for the surgical team to remove all of the affected area and reconstruct a new esophagus from a section of colon. Uncertainty became almost overpowering as minutes turned into hours and hours into a day. And still the endless waiting continued as two friends from home sat at her side. A nurse intermittently came out to report progress and assured the continued extension of time indicated progress was being made behind the swinging doors.

The extreme mugginess of August added to Kathy's tension. Thoughts repeatedly returned home. How would this upheaval affect her girls' futures with all stability suddenly turned upside down? Life—so simple, serene and secure one moment—in the next breath can become pandemonium. Like cancer itself, life is terminal. She realized they could only take one moment at a time—nothing more.

As day drew into night, the doctor emerged tired and exhausted. Sam was alive, but the cancer had spread beyond the esophagus and into surrounding glands. Weakening vital signs and human limitations forced the team to stop. "I'm sorry I couldn't finish the operation," he began and wearily described the procedure. They had been forced to remove most of the stomach except the duodenum, the esophagus, spleen, and surrounding lymph glands. The blood supply and section of colon were cut off to force the section to strengthen. In a later operation, it would become an esophagus. For now, Sam would be kept alive by an integral food pump inserted into the small intestine. From an opening in Sam's neck, sputum would drip into a small bag. Months would go by without Sam tasting food.

Sam's post-op recovery was often horrifying and frightening but miraculously successful. "I couldn't have made it without Kathy," said Sam. "She was there day and night, never leaving my side. She was my strength and my hope." Many times a tight handclasp was the only available communication as life-giving hope flowed from one to another.

Sam was released to fly home a week ahead of schedule accompanied by the food pump and his competent and unswerving nurse, Kathy. For the next three months he could have absolutely nothing by mouth, and the pump had to be connected twenty to twenty-four hours a day. Its proper function was absolutely vital to life. "I didn't miss eating so much, but I would have given anything for a drink of water," recalled Sam. There is only One who fully understands the extremity of such suffering.

Now there was no other choice than to keep going forward. Somehow they would see it through. Contemplating the completion of Sam's operation stirred mixed emotions. Returning to Omaha would be difficult, but it had to be done. Sam longed to feel whole and fully alive again, yet he prepared for the ordeal with great apprehension.

The fateful day arrived. Highly skilled hands removed the prepared section of colon and attached it to the two remaining inches of esophagus at the throat. The other end was then attached to the duodenum that would serve as the stomach. The final step was to reconnect the lower colon and remove the sputum bag at Sam's neck.

Following another painful recovery, Sam began to feel miraculously whole. He was now able to sit up a few hours a day and take small meals. How glorious was Thanksgiving Day as Sam carefully sampled the hospital's holiday dinner! How glorious indeed was life.

For the first time in over three months, Sam was able to physically participate in the sacrament as the missionaries prepared the ordinance in his hospital room. Unspoken words of gratitude streamed forth in grateful tears as covenants were renewed. Again the witness of the Lord's promise "to always be with (him)" burned within Sam's breast. And he would yet need His continued presence.

Homecoming

Joy and gratitude, along with the food pump (still attached for nutritional backup)—accompanied Sam and Kathy as they returned home. Or was it heaven that greeted them with smiling faces and grateful hearts? This holiday season witnessed again the miracle of life, and a special sacredness attended the Matthews' home as they celebrated the birth of Him whom they had learned to love and know so well.

. The new year was greeted with a resolve to never again take anything for granted. This newly offered and now fully appreciated gift of time would be used to strengthen family and prepare for tomorrow. Life indeed was joyous in spite of its sorrow and trials! Understanding and appreciating such a fragile gift insured it would now be used wisely.

Home at last returned to normal as church assignments, school, work, and dance lessons filled a busy schedule. Melodies ringing from the piano, the aroma of fresh hot cookies, and most noticeably children's laughter filled the air. Adversity would surely knock no more.

"We Cannot Change the Wind, but We Can Adjust Our Sails"

The spring found Sam doing remarkably well, but Kathy was suffering with a perplexing and many times excruciating pain in her lower back. She visited the doctor anticipating some help so she could go on with things, but instead test results brought disheartening news.

The breast cancer was back and had masticized in Kathy's lower back. She numbly listened as he explained that it had not really returned but had always been there—inactive. How could this be? She had done everything they had told her to do. She had taken the chemo for a year when she could have stopped at nine months. She had been as positive as she knew how to be. "So why now, after four years and all we've been through? How much more will the Lord require of me? Of us?" The questions repeated themselves.

Kathy would continue to live, to face endless tests and unpleasant treatment and remain strong within. "I used to think we lived for a cure. Now I know we live for today, as fully as possible, and appreciate what we have," Kathy counseled.

Today Sam and Kathy conquer the unconquerable by not allowing it to destroy them within. Their philosophy, "It may destroy this body, but it will not destroy me," gives dignity to an unmerciful disease.

So simple a thing, so strong a hand,
Hand of the Creator
Hand that serves
Hand that lifts and reaches or the
Hand that suffers
They are all one. [1]

If you were to visit the Pingree Ward on Sunday, you would be welcomed at the chapel door by cheerful and smiling door greeters, Sam and Kathy. Your hand would be clasped in unconditional love, fellowship, and deep understanding. Shining eyes would meet yours, and a calm and motivating spirit would lift you. For they and their children have learned that those who wish to sing always find a song.

---

[1] Dorothy Casper, 1989

CHAPTER EIGHT

Higher Flight Levels

Scott

"The higher we soar, the farther we see."

Late January of 1987 I felt like a "born-again" senior as I sat in seminary on Bishop's Day. Our class listened intently as area priesthood leaders counselled us. And then my own bishop, whom I loved dearly, stood. I struggled to swallow the lump that welled in my throat and blinked hard to conceal tears as he began to read from a letter I recognized.

Why Change?

"Have you ever felt that life was meaningless? Have you ever thought that things aren't going right for you? Does it seem like one minute you are doing great and the next minute nothing works? I don't know if this applies to anyone except myself, but I will tell you a story about me.

"All through my high school years . . . I would do what everybody else did. It would seem great for awhile, but I knew it wasn't right. My conscience would bother me, but I would put it at the back of my mind until it quit pestering me.

"Church was another thing. It always seemed so boring that I could hardly stand it. I never read my scriptures and when I did try, they seemed like a bunch of words on a page that didn't mean anything. Seminary was the only thing that I did like to attend.

"One day, I just sat around the house and everything seemed depressing. Everything seemed pointless. *What is the meaning of life? Why are we here?* I thought about it awhile. Then I decided to change my outlook on life. I slowly started to repent and even started praying.

"Eventually, I began to study the scriptures, and suddenly they seemed more interesting. I could relate to some of the stories and see the principles that were trying to be put across. My whole attitude changed. Church seemed better, and I broke my yearly line of absence in my Sunday School class. Everything started getting better and I even felt better.

"Now I know that there is a difference between living bad and trying to live right. I encourage all who read this to try to live better, and soon things that once angered you or depressed you will hardly bother you anymore. You feel good about yourself and you think positive. . . . Living the gospel is a lot better.

Even though I felt conspicuous and kind of on the spot, the Spirit burned within my heart as he read *my words* to the class. I evaluated it carefully as he spoke, and it did sound pretty good. But more importantly, I hoped it would help someone who was struggling for a testimony.

I had been the bishop's priest quorum assistant and a few weeks earlier during a visit in his office, I told him about the changes that had come into my life since school had started. It just kind of poured out of me, and when I finished he asked if I would be willing to write it down so it could maybe help others. I have been keeping a journal, too, so I'd like to invite you to go back into a few of my entries and let me explain how it started for me.

Journal November 23, 1986 [1]

"Today, I felt like I needed to change my ways and try to become better. I have tried a few times in the past, but I always seemed to not quite make it. I had this *feeling* that things just weren't going right. Outwardly they seemed fine. I had a great football season, and I made All-conference in football as a linebacker. My grades weren't too bad—they were better than last year's. But *something* was missing.

"I started to read the Book of Mormon. I had started many times in the past, but each time it soon became boring, and I would quit. My seminary teacher made the Book of Mormon clearer, and this time I was determined to read it. At first my seminary teacher and I didn't get along very well. I always talked to the girl next to me, and he would get mad.

"I sluffed with some football players one day and he found out. He wanted to kick me out of seminary, and I was furious! The next day I decided to talk to him about it. We had a lengthy talk in which he told me the only reason he had come down so hard on me and not the other people, was (because I) was like the 'leader' of the class, and people looked up to me as an example of being 'cool.' After that things got better, and now he is one of the best teachers that I have ever had. Anyway, I began to read the Book of Mormon, and I also began to pray and ask the Lord for help with my problems, and to help me *understand the meaning of life*."

November 24, 1986

"This morning I started out with prayer. I figured it couldn't hurt. I tried to clean up my language, although that habit is hard to break. Nevertheless, I cut back considerably. It is night, and I just got through reading my scriptures. I decided not to play D&D (Dungeons and Dragons) anymore. That was one of the few things that I had disagreed with the Church on, so I decided to quit. I think I'll say my prayers now."

November 25, 1986

"Today wasn't too bad—I woke up and said my prayers and then went to school. Then I came home and had an estimate to have my car painted. The guy wanted $600.00 and I buy the paint!!!

That's probably when I made a mental note that I would have to ask for a paint job for graduation. I had worked hard every summer moving pipe and driving truck in harvest, but I still couldn't afford to finish the car. Dad and I had built it together. We put three cars together, and I did nearly everything myself except putting in the motor. We started it in my junior year, and it took nearly nine months to finish it. I was so glad to have it but almost too embarrassed to drive it! You see, it was still the colors of the three original cars—red, green, and brown. Dad said if I got on the honor roll and stayed on it, he would buy the insurance, and I could drive it to school. So I did. I found it surprisingly not too hard once I decided to do it. When the folks asked why I hadn't gotten A's before I said, 'I don't know. . . . I just didn't.' Anyway, that was the last entry into my journal for 1986.

I was born in San Leandro, California, the third child of Richard and Maurine Stocking. I came along as a surprise and Mom says a blessing, too. She already had my two older brothers, Dennis, eight, and Brett, five, and the odds were 99 to 1 that she wouldn't have another child. When Mom discovered she was expecting me, the doctors also discovered she had cancer. After I was born, they were able to take care of it, and Mom has always said I saved her life. Maybe we both gave each other life. Anyway, she has sure been a neat Mom to me.

Mom worked when I was little, and for the first

three years of my life, Dad tended me during the days and then worked at night. He did everything for me and took care of all my needs. He even put a little seat on his bicycle and took me everywhere, even to a job interview at a large nuclear energy company. They must have liked him (and me too) because he got the job.

We moved to Moreland, Idaho, when I was eight years old. I had never seen snow before and I was so excited. When the canal froze over, I skated on the ice all day and then ran into the house exclaiming, 'This is the best day of my life!'"

Once I entered a Mother's Day essay contest. I wrote:

"My mom is very special to me for all kinds of things she does for me. She is special because she is someone I can talk to if I had a bad test score or did something wrong. When I talk to her, she understands the problem and won't get mad.

"My mom will stick with me when the going gets tough. When I am lonely she will accompany me so I will be happy again. When I am sick, she will keep me home from school or keep me from playing. My mom is special because she loves me and nothing will stop her from loving me. She is special to me because I am her son, and *nothing will change that forever.*"

I won the contest! And Mom said it was her happiest day, too.

Mom gave me life, and Dad saved it when I was three. He was a navy plane captain and an excellent scuba diver and liked to take us three boys drift-fishing for stripers in the San Pablo Bay. One day a friend of Dad's and Dennis and Brett and I were out in Dad's little boat. A large party boat passed by too closely causing water to come into our hull. Dad started bailing with a little bucket, but when the waves came over the side, he hollered for us to jump clear. Dad was the only one without a life jacket. The boat started to go down and then it suddenly flipped upside down. As I tried to jump clear, my lifejacket got snagged on the frame, and I was trapped beneath the boat. Dad and I were both underwater as he worked frantically to release me. He said he yanked and yanked for what seemed like an eternity knowing I would drown in seconds. He finally freed me, and we surfaced. Another boat had picked up the others but couldn't reach us in the choppy water. Dad was so tired that his legs began cramping, and they were so numb that he couldn't swim. We bobbed helplessly in the water together, and Dad intended to let go of me if my little jacket started to sink. Somehow he managed to propel us to the rescue boat, and we were pulled to safety. He said I never cried. Even in treacherous ocean water at the age of three, I must have felt safe with Dad.

I was "lucky" another time when I was eleven. We had been cleaning the yard early that spring, and the branches we pruned were kind of green, so I poured gasoline on them to make them burn. I hadn't noticed that gas had dripped from the can as I backed up, and when I threw a match into the pile, the fire quickly streaked up the trail I had accidentally dripped. When I saw it coming straight for me, I stuck my foot over the gas can to prevent it from exploding, and before I knew what happened the fire had come up my legs. Dad had taught me to roll if I ever caught on fire, and I did. There were second- and third-degree burns on my legs, but for some reason I never scarred.

Junior high years came along, and I decided to try my hand at musical theatre. They said my blonde hair and blue eyes and cheesy grin were perfect for the part, and I got the lead in *Charlie Brown*. Besides singing, I liked snow skiing and sports, and once I won a pie-eating contest. I only had one merit badge left, but I never did finish my Eagle. Back then I never gave much thought to grades or my future, but I began to see things more clearly my senior year.

In English we were required to write a paper entitled, 'What is the Most Important Thing to Tell a Freshman?' so I wrote:

"It has come to my attention that the eighth graders will need advice about their upcoming high school years. Being a senior and about to graduate, I would like to leave you with some advice. When I was a freshman, I didn't think about grades or activities. I thought I would have plenty of time to make choices. The time to start working is now. It is very important to prepare for scholarships; colleges require a copy of your grades from your freshman year through your senior year. If you are serious about college, start studying now."

Although I didn't decide to do well in school until kind of late, I always loved to read and learn.

Years ago, Dad made me a deal that he would buy any book I wanted to read. That deal cost him a lot of money! Ever week I went to the bookstore and picked something out and I belonged to several book clubs. Science fiction was my favorite, and I decided in high school that someday I would write a book.

I went out for football my junior year and played on the JV team, and the coach let me suit up for the varsity, too. Being 5'8" and weighing only 130 lbs., size and lack of experience were against me. But towards the end of the season, the coach let me play the last quarter and my senior year I played both offense and defense. Over the summer I had put on 35 lbs., and I was ready for a great season and a lot of action. That year I was running back and became the kickoff man and also the field goal kicker. One of the neatest honors I ever received was being chosen as All-State Conference Linebacker. Dad really got a kick out of reading about me in the sports sections of the local newspapers after games. I gave it my all and loved it!

Dad never missed a game. I remember once we played in the rain, and there were no spectators except Dad. I was so embarrassed because he was out there in the pouring rain walking back and forth hollering and cheering for us. He was always there for me. Another time he drove from Salmon to see me play in the Mini-Dome. I didn't think he could come, but I kept checking the grandstand. I didn't know he was there until the team bus got home and then I drove the six hours back to Salmon with him. We had kind of a neat thing going. Whenever I wanted to really talk to Dad, I would reach over and turn the radio down. He got the signal and was ready to listen. Never did he question my word, and I knew he trusted me.

Football was first priority in my life. For an assignment on priorities I wrote:

"The most important thing a high school student can do is play football. (I guess girls were excluded.) Football practice develops the player physically, and football practice develops the player mentally. It is exciting to play against another school, and the feeling of winning is great, but it's the *practice that makes the player good.*"

I decided my senior year to "practice" living better, and it changed my life! This is how I felt the winter of my senior year when I was seventeen.

January 18, 1987

"It has been a few days since I wrote last so I will sum it up. During the month of December I faced many trials . . . and I struggled with many problems. Towards the end of the month I began to get stronger in facing my trials. I made a New Year's resolution to start the new year with a new attitude. Since then, the Lord has blessed me greatly. I am finding it easier to do good, and I am on the road to repentance.

"I finished the Book of Mormon in the early days of January, and I am starting it again so I can get the full meaning of the scriptures. Last Sunday I gave a talk in church about missionary work. That was when I decided on a mission for sure. *1987 is my year. It is a year to prepare fully* for my mission. . . . It seems like time just slips away and never slows for anyone. You have to be ready to face it.

"Today I received a recommend for a patriarchal blessing. Thus I end this day's recording."

February 1, 1987

"I have finally gotten my patriarchal blessing. The feeling I had when I received it on the 25th is almost indescribable. I felt elevated and pure. My head felt light, and I could sense the presence of the Holy Ghost. A few days after that, I received it written. The Lord has many things in store for me if I remain righteous. It says I will serve a mission if I am worthy. It tells me to be careful and live my life for those who follow. (I didn't fully realize then what that meant.) It tells me that I will be a leader and people will call me 'Blessed' for my example. . . . (it) also says that I will be able to increase my faith. That proves to me that the Lord was really talking to me because I have been praying for greater faith.

"I know the gospel is true and that the Book of Mormon is true. I hope and pray I can always be faithful to the Lord and always remember Him. I want to learn so much about the gospel, and *now it seems like there isn't enough time to learn all that I need to know.*

"I made the Honor Roll . . for the first time and I know I did it with the Lord's help. I hope my friends will follow my example and yearn for the gospel. . . I've about summed everything up so I will end now. AMEN."

February 8, 1987

"Today was Sunday, and I have already started getting things from my blessing. I am being made president of my seminary class for the rest of the year. It doesn't sound like much, but I know it is a step to prepare me for the future.

"Today there was a stake priesthood meeting. This is the first time I had gone to one, and I really liked it and wished I had gone in the past. I am really confused about what I should do for a career and for the rest of my life."

I really was concerned about the future, and shortly after graduation, I read an article in a Scouting magazine about flying. It indicated it was an open field with a lot of opportunity. Mom and I talked about the future and what I should do with my life many times, and she suggested that I look into aviation when I got to BYU in the fall. She advised me to take general classes and wait until after my mission to make a decision because I would have a much clearer outlook then.

Fall came and leaving home was the *toughest* thing I had ever had to do. You won't believe this, but I called home four times the first day!! The first few months away were quite an adjustment to say the very least.

September 7, 1987

"Wow! It's been a long time since I have written . . . I grew close to my family over the summer, and it really hurt when I left for college. Dennis and I are like best friends, and I am really homesick and miss home every minute. It helps when I can call and talk to Mom and Dad. Being away from home and by myself makes me see how much I love my family and home. *I hope we can all live worthily to live forever together.*

"I am so confused about a major and a career. I am taking flying lessons, and I hope to get my pilot's license by Christmas. I am asking the Lord for help to decide my future.

"I am lost at this college, but maybe I can adjust soon.

"I got my recommendation for advancement in the Melchizedek Priesthood last Sunday, and over Labor Day weekend I got to go home and go bear hunting with Dennis and Dad. It felt so good to be home even though I was only gone a week and a half! I returned to Provo tired but determined to do my best and adjust to do well in school."

September 9, 1987
"Today I took my first math test. I think I did O.K. I don't feel so homesick anymore, although I still miss home. I'm trying to live worthy, and it doesn't seem as hard anymore. It seems like it is time to start growing up now. I hope I can make the transition easily."

September 12, 1987
"Today seemed better than yesterday. It almost seems fun around here. I received a 71% on the math

test, so now I'm going to study harder. I am about to
solo in flying lessons. Right now I have nine hours of
flight. Maybe I can get a job flying someday."

I loved flying lessons, getting up in the air and
flying around the area helped me relax and get away
from the stress. It was a chance to think about life in
general and put things into perspective. Someone once
said that the higher we soar the farther we see. *That
not only goes for flying, but also for living.*

September 29, 1987

"It's Tuesday night, and I just came back from
the movie *The Lord of the Flies*. What a bomb! I soloed
last week and have been trying to catch up on the book
work for written aviation exams. I also have to get
ready for tests coming up next week. Last week I took
another math test and received a 78%. I still need to
study harder."

Just as in football, you have to practice to
improve. I tried hard to not be discouraged but just
kept practicing to do better. I'm trying to be the best I
can be.

October 11, 1987

"Today is Sunday, and I've been pretty busy. I
went home last weekend to help pack out a bear, but
the thing was just a shrimp so we didn't shoot it. I took
another math test and got a 105%. That helped my
grade a lot. We did our home teaching today. Lately
I've been wanting to start a book . . . maybe I will when

I get my pilot license."

October 18, 1987
"President Benson came Tuesday, and I had the seat on the back row on the floor. He seemed really cool, and he talked on morality. I flew my cross-country to Logan yesterday, and it was really fun. I still can't decide what to major in or what to do in life. I hope the Lord will help me answer those questions because I know that *He knows what would be best for me*. I'm hoping that a mission will help me to evaluate myself, my goals, and my future."

November 15, 1987
"Well, it's Sunday again, and I felt like writing . . . I'm trying to do well in school, but it seems hard. I hope I can improve my study habits. I'm thinking about going into the R.O.T.C. program and entering the Air Force as an officer and trying to become a pilot.

"I went home last week and was made an elder. I hope I can be worthy to represent the Lord. When I look back on this in twenty years, I want to *remember (how I felt) now*."

There were several of us presented at stake conference to become elders. My birthday isn't for eight more months, but I have such a strong desire to be ordained and prepare myself for a mission the following spring. As we came off the stand after conference, everyone shook our hands congratulating us and asked where our calls were to. When they asked me, I smiled and said, "Oh, I don't have a call."

My next visit home was for Thanksgiving. The folks had planned to go to California but postponed it for a week because I couldn't go with them. We had a great time. My friends, and I watched fifteen videos! That has to be a record! I just couldn't seem to get a clear answer about my future, and Mom and I talked it over again. I said, "Mom, maybe I won't have to worry so much about the future. I believe that the Second Coming of Christ is going to be so soon that I won't have to worry about a career." She said she didn't think it was *that* soon, but somehow *I felt it was very near.*

Every time I came home from college in my car—which was now one color (blue), Dad would fill up the gas tank for me and give me forty dollars, in two twenties, so I would have extra money if I needed it. I had the habit of carrying five dollars in my wallet and Dad would tell me over and over it wasn't enough. The hard part came every time I had to leave. I always put on my sunglasses even if it was cloudy so they wouldn't see my tears. But I think they were probably "on to me." We loved each other so much, and yet we had never been verbally open about expressing our feelings. The first time I had to leave, Dad put out his hand to shake mine and in a husky voice, with sunglasses hiding my tears I said, "I don't shake hands. We hug." And we embraced then and always after as we parted.

I surprised my parents on a special trip home the first part of December. I came in the plane instead of the car and proudly called them from the airport and said, "Hey, how about picking me up?" Were they ever surprised and pleased that I had soloed home. The only problem was that it was a cold, stormy day. The wind had really picked up in Idaho, and Dad, being an experienced plane captain, was concerned that I had landed in forty-mile-an-hour winds.

They took me home for a short visit, and when we walked through the front door, I started going through the things they had just brought home from California. I was thrilled that they had bought a video camera, and we took pictures of everyone. I noticed a new backpack that appeared to be made just for me, and I showed Mom how good it looked as I modelled it for her. She said it was supposed to be a Christmas present, but to go ahead and take it with me. So I got in on Christmas a little early.

At the airport, Dad videoed me and watched carefully as I went through the pre-flight checklist. I promised to call and let them know I had made it safely. Then with sunglasses intact, once again to hide the tears, we all hugged good-bye, and I took off into the clouds as Dad videoed me.

I called from Provo as soon as I got to the apartment. They said that when I tipped my wings as I flew out of sight, it really frightened Mom. But Dad told her I was waving good-bye. I said, "That wasn't a wave. I was fighting the wind!" But wave or not, my heart was always with them. They were relieved that I had made it okay, and Dad asked about the practice touch and go's I made in Ogden. I told him not to worry so much because if anything ever went wrong, I could land on the interstate.

Then before we hung up, I kind of choked up and

said, "Dad, . . . I've got something to tell you." He replied, "What's that, Scott?" I said, "I love you, Dad." I could tell he was at a loss for words, and there were a few seconds of silence. Tears ran down my cheeks as over the phone I heard him say, "I love you, too, Scott."

Before I went to bed that December 6, 1987, I wrote in my journal about my wonderful trip home and the special visit with my family. My entry continues:

"The semester is almost over and right now I feel pretty good about my grades. I hope I can get at least a 3.5 or better. I can't wait for this semester to be over. Pretty soon I'll be on my mission. The major question about a career hasn't been answered yet. I am hoping the time I spend on my mission will help clear it up.

"It's almost Christmas. I went to the mall, and it was packed. It seems like the Christmas spirit has been lost in money madness. Well, I guess that's enough for awhile.

"I'm a few flight hours away from my license. Hopefully, by next entry, I'll have it."

Another busy week followed, and on Monday, December 14, Scott flew another three hours, and his requirements were nearly completed. He had taken the written exam the week before and earned one of the highest scores ever attained in the state of Utah.

Everyone at the flying school loved Scott. They didn't even know at the time he was a student at the

"Y." He always just wore jeans and a clean shirt and never appeared "preppy" or superior. He was especially admired by his instructor, who drilled Scott repeatedly as they flew, preparing him for his final flight on Wednesday. He said that Scott had mastered the materials so well, and his skills were so keen that he could no longer stump him. But occasionally Scott could "stump" him.

That Monday as Scott returned from his three-hour flight, his instructor called and asked if Scott would like to fly back up to Salt Lake. Always eager for a chance to fly, Scott said, "Sure!"

At the Salt Lake Airport, a charter pilot who was returning a Piper Warrior plane to Provo invited Scott to fly with him. Interested in seeing how a low-wing handled compared to the plane he flew, Scott gladly took the other front seat as a passenger. Just before 7 p.m. they took off headed south, but as they reached the Draper area, the engine malfunctioned, and they immediately lost power. Radioing "May Day" and following emergency procedures, they began shutting down the equipment, including the lights to prevent fire on impact.

Interstate 15 southbound lane was directly below and full of traffic. Not wanting to cause an accident for motorists, they banked hard to the left attempting to land on the less busy northbound lane. Both worked quickly and concentrated on bringing it down. But in the darkness the nose gear, just two feet too low, clipped an unseen power line that stood some twenty feet higher than the rest of the embankment.

Flashes of electricity filled the sky as witnesses
on the ground and Scott's friend and instructor flying
directly behind them saw the plane flip over and crash
upside down. A nurse was among the first at the scene
to offer assistance, but Scott had been killed instantly.
The pilot died two days later in an area hospital.

When a sheriff's deputy knocked at the door of
the Stocking home that night, Scott's father knew
immediately that he was there because of Scott.

Grief-stricken parents visited Scott's apartment
at BYU and bathed with tears his personal belongings.
There they found an envelope containing several
twenty dollar bills, the exact amount Richard had
given to his son on his weekend departures. He had
probably been saving it for Christmas presents. Among
his books and school assignments were papers he had
written for different classes expressing many of his
beliefs and desires. Most cherished of all was the
personal journal that no one knew Scott kept. It was
from these items and experiences shared by Richard
and Maurine that Scott's story has been *carefully
constructed* and hopefully shared as he would have
desired.

Someone once said that every man's life is a
diary in which he means to write one thing, but
actually writes another. His finest hour comes when
he compares the volume *as it is* with the one that he
vowed he would make it. Scott's finest hour has come,
and his volumes are complete. His example has shown
us how to meet life and live it to its fullest.

An obscure boy, unknown to the world, from a little community in southeastern Idaho lived so much like another teacher in an obscure village long ago, one whom Scott knew and tried to emulate. Perhaps he has written his book, after all.

---

1 All personal journal entries have been edited from Scott Stocking's personal journal as dated. Permission granted by Richard and Maurine Stocking.

CHAPTER NINE

A New Day Dawning

Carol and Dayle

"We mount to heaven mostly on the ruins of our cherished schemes."
A. B. Alcott

It has been said that death is the greatest sorrow, sin the greatest burden, and debt the greatest bondage. Faith-promoting stories and testimonies are often borne by those who have experienced and overcome the great trials of sin and the sorrow of death. These witnesses offer hope, comfort, and courage to others who struggle. Unfortunately, far less frequent are accounts of people who have experienced the terrible bondage of financial disaster and debt. Shame, remorse, and loneliness are many times constant companions of those who feel alone and trapped by their own mistakes.

A highly respected and well-loved man had for years enjoyed a somewhat affluent lifestyle produced from the labor of his hands. But in later years, he suffered sizeable losses and financial bondage. Self-doubt and lessened worth surfaced as this kind and gentle man tearfully said, "I think I could accept illness or a death or some other problem as a test or an interruption in life. But this? Losing everything I've worked all my life for? It's hard to feel that it's a trial or test and not just the consequences of my own foolishness."

For many, these are difficult economic times. In the midst of business failure, layoffs, and unemployment lines, making ends meet has become increasingly difficult. We know well the lessons learned from earning our bread by the sweat of our brow as the Lord intended. Life was not meant to be easy, and our trials are often compounded because so many of us simply make mistakes. And so it has always been that we learn from our mistakes to know good from evil. Surely Joseph Smith, Sr. felt discouragement and failure as he moved his family from homestead to homestead trying to survive. During such trying times, he trained within the walls of his humble home a boy prophet whose life would change history.

A century later another great man erred in financial judgment. In 1920, David O. McKay, then an Apostle, and his brother, Thomas, were encouraged by

Church members to invest in a cotton development in
Arizona that promised big dividends. Each brother
borrowed large amounts of money and put up their
lands in Huntsville as collateral. The project collapsed,
and the two lost their entire investment. The money
raised in local banks could not be secured even if the
farms were sold.

Dismal days followed as they met the crisis. Both
lived with financial strain and worry for some thirty
years until all of the debt was repaid. They had made
an honest transaction that had failed. Meanwhile
David would continue to serve the Lord in the public
eye as a General Authority. Few would know of the
financial stress and weight he carried.[1]

When we make mistakes or have difficult times,
we need to realize that we are not alone. All who have
felt the clutches of overwhelming debt and the
subsequent lost agency know feelings of foolishness
and unworthiness. We have been counselled all of our
lives to avoid debt. Our leaders have warned of its
enormous toll on lives and families, and yet so many
cross the line, too often ignorant of the torment
awaiting them. It is then, trapped and imprisoned,
they feel foolish and their lives wasted.

The painful lessons we learn from today's
interruptions prepare us for tomorrow. It is on dark
days that we learn the most. Keats said, "Failure is . . .
the highway to success, inasmuch as every discovery of

[1]Keith Terry, *David O. McKay, Prophet of Love* (Orem, UT: Butterfly,
Inc. 1980), pp. 60-61.

what is false leads us to seek earnestly after what is
true, and every fresh experience points out to some
form of error which we shall afterward carefully
avoid."[2]

On November 29, 1983, Elder M. Russell Ballard
at a Devotional Address at BYU, counselled students to
"think straight" and develop good judgment in all
areas of life. He then courageously shared a painful
experience in his life when he failed to "think
straight."

As a young businessman, Elder Ballard was
encouraged to become the Salt Lake City Edsel dealer
for the Ford Motor Company. The Edsel proved to be
one of the most disastrous national marketing
mistakes in the history of the United States. Ford spent
over two hundred million dollars producing a car that
would carry the name of Edsel Ford, the father of
Henry Ford.

Elder Ballard wrestled with his decision and
decided he wanted to see the car before signing the
franchise. The Ford Motor Company made special
arrangements and flew Elder Ballard and his father to
California. It was a big decision involving a lot of
money, and Elder Ballard was earnestly asking for the
Lord's direction.

The minute Elder Ballard saw the car he had the
distinct impression not to go ahead with the franchise.

---

[2] J. Spencer Kinard, *A Time for Reflection* from *The Spoken Word*
(Salt Lake City, UT: Deseret Book, 1986), p. 27.

But when he left the car show, the Ford Motor Company started working on him again, assuring him that it would be a great success. And he weakened and drifted from the Spirit's promptings. The rest is painful history. He signed the franchise and then went through "the torments of the damned" almost. He shared with the students that it is no fun to lose a lot of money fast. Regardless of what he did, he couldn't stop the losses. He ultimately sold the franchise at a great loss.

"I think straight now when it comes to those kinds of decisions because of what I suffered. Perhaps we need to understand that failure is a part of life. We are not going to be successful in everything we do, but we never need to fail to learn the lesson and to place in the bank of our memories those things that will then cause us to become increasingly powerful, and most importantly, increasingly helpful to the building of the kingdom of God."3

We need to remember the lessons learned from our mistakes and then let go of the past. Wounds and scars from such physical and spiritual bondage are deep and painful. Financial entrapment literally changes lives and personalities. Long after the shackles of bondage loosen their grip, an anguished soul cries out:

---

3 *BYU Fireside and Devotional Speeches* (Provo, UT: BYU Press, 1983-84), p. 36.

Free Me

Take from me the pain and anger and leave me,
As I Once was:
Void of fear and sorrow—
Full of joy and love.

Take from me the weary lines
That etch my face.
Heal them, and remove the calloused ruts
That mar my soul.

Cast away this hardened shell, and let me feel
As I once did.
Erase the grudge within my heart—mend the scars
That I conceal.

Take from me the past.
Give to me the Future.
Grant me courage to be whole, and faith
To dream again.[4]

How grateful we are for those in life who are
willing to share lessons learned from judgment they
later regretted. Dayle and Carol Holm today are
successful and happy and appear to have few
problems, but once they walked the painful and lonely

---

4 Marilyn Whyte, *Free Me*, 1989.

road of bondage. They know and now live the laws of financial success. Dayle owns and operates an excavation business, and Carol is successful in the insurance and investment business holding both a C.L.U. and C.H.F.C. But it was not always so.

A well-known financial planner and gifted public speaker, Carol is frequently asked to speak to church and community groups. Her extended empathy and understanding for those struggling in painful remorse repeatedly lifts, comforts, and inspires. On one occasion, she was asked to conduct a workshop on financial difficulties at a stake women's conference. Checking the bookstores and back issues of Church magazines for resource materials, she found there was nothing published on going broke. Many articles and books were available on financial planning and business management, but nothing on coping with economic failure. Carol realized that someone needed to deal with those emotions and share them openly. Many lives have been strengthened as she has courageously shared her experiences. She and Dayle know first-hand that it is one of the most dangerous things a couple can experience.

Carol grew up the fifth of seven children on a dairy farm just east of Idaho Falls. The family worked hard and shared more love than money during those years. Carol was a happy, outgoing child surrounded by many friends. When her older brother, eight years her senior, graduated from school, Carol made the decision to help her dad with the chores. She preferred the outdoors and really didn't mind milking morning and night.

A sunny disposition and endless energy drew everyone to her. Known as everyone's "Sunshine Girl," being happy came easy to Carol. She tackled everything that came along and usually came out on top. The saying under her senior picture, "She could sell you something you didn't even know you wanted," aptly described her exuberant and infectious nature. After graduation, she worked as a dental assistant and saved for college.

It was no wonder that Dayle, a handsome and very sought-after returned missionary, was immediately attracted to her. He had also lived in the Ammon area and was even a fifth cousin to this bubbly blonde. Being five years older, he had never really noticed her until he returned from a two-and-a-half-year-mission in Sweden. Dayle had enjoyed more of the finer pleasures of life than his sweetheart, but he also knew hard work and discipline from the schedule of life on a dairy farm. At the time, his family operated the largest Grade A dairy in the upper Snake River Valley. He and Carol courted for one year and two months and then were married in the Idaho Falls Temple.

As newlyweds, it seemed everything they touched turned to gold. From combined savings, they purchased their first home, just prior to their wedding. Both had been working in a photography shop in Blackfoot, and after six months they confidently approached the owner desiring to go into competition or buy his business. He admired their ambition and

decided to sell. Business was good and everything went
great, so a year and a half later they bought a bigger
and nicer home when their first child was born.
During this period they became involved with Dale
Carnegie classes, and it became a turning point in
their lives. "We felt we could accomplish anything,"
Dayle said. They enjoyed selling and teaching
Carnegie classes as graduate assistants. They loved it,
and their schedule became so demanding they hired a
manager for the photography shop. Soon, both desired
a bigger challenge, and they decided to sell. One year
later, the new owner went broke and instead of a
payment, they received a bankruptcy notice and were
out four thousand dollars.

Undaunted and filled with faith in hard work
and a positive attitude, they next became involved in a
marble manufacturing company in Idaho Falls. It
never really got off the ground, and Dayle traded his
stocks for shares in a beauty business. The next twelve
years would teach many aspects of this unknown field
to young and ambitious kids. They moved to Idaho
Falls, and for the next five years managed a beauty
supply house owned by Dayle and his dad, and they did
very well. The future looked bright as their accountant
advised that steady growth at the present rate would
insure success.

Their next major step came when two national
companies wanted them to expand and cover the entire
state of Idaho, threatening to withdraw their product
lines (Zotos and Redkin). Dayle and Carol made an
emotional decision to do whatever was necessary to

keep from losing those product lines. Hindsight is very good, but at the time, they didn't realize that they just didn't have the capital to pull off the expansion. They were involved with motivational seminars three times a week, and positive thinking overshadowed judgment. Carol commented, "Sometimes I think it's dangerous to have such positive attitudes and be so young and naive. The positive takes over and there's nothing there saying, 'Wait a minute, we don't have enough money to pull this off.'"

Young and inexperienced, they reached for the opportunity and expanded statewide, opening three new stores in Pocatello, Twin Falls, and Boise. A second child was born, followed by a move to Boise. There they invested in a beautiful new home, bought an expensive sports car, and purchased a cabin lot at Cascade. The business grew and became so large two years later that Dayle and Carol realized they would either have to hire more salesmen and expand or sell. Things had gotten tighter and tighter, so when an interested buyer came along, they sold and moved back to Idaho Falls with their two small children.

Although they realized they had really lost ground financially, they had always been so good at landing on their feet that they were far from discouraged. Dayle was able to get enough money from the Boise sale to make a down payment on a beauty college in Idaho Falls, and soon their third child was born. They employed eight beauticians and taught about thirty students. Carol worked as the receptionist for the next two years. Dayle was well trained with the

Redkin Company and lectured at area hair colleges and at ISU. The business did well and provided an adequate income.

Being ambitious and not having a full schedule, Dayle got a part-time job selling motorcycles and snowmobiles at the Suzuki shop. The owner interested him in buying a store of his own in Blackfoot. They found a man willing to build the building and give them a long-term lease. Raising five thousand dollars for a parts kit, they opened the new business with tremendous overhead and very little capital. Suzuki floored all the machines, and the Holms again moved to Blackfoot enthused about their new opportunity.

The first fall, motorcycles sales were great and success appeared inevitable. However, the energy crisis and gas scare the following winter left snowmobiles sitting on the showroom floor to be carried over for another year. Three light snowfall years complicated the problem. Dayle could never recover in the summer months the losses he accrued during the winters. For four years he struggled but then owed so much money to Suzuki that he became "out of trust."

The company finally came and took the remainder of their machines and then rejected three potential buyers who had wanted the business. Before, the young couple had always been able to sell and get out of their problems gracefully without anyone on the outside knowing. But this time they couldn't. The next two years became a nightmare as Dayle even tried selling used machines and cars on the lot of what had become a second-hand store.

"I did whatever I could do to survive. I didn't think about failure, but there were times that I was really down," said Dayle. "The day they took the cycle I remember thinking, 'If I ever get out of this, I'll never be unhappy again.' I've lived up to the promise I made that dark day. And it's never been that bad again."

Dayle had slipped into inactivity during the years he owned the cycle shop. The store sponsored a racing team, and he was gone every weekend racing. Carol had been secretly praying that Dayle's priorities would change and that he would become active again. And he did. The stake presidency called him to the stake Young Men's presidency. They expressed their admiration for his desire to fight and never give up. Dayle had never considered his situation in that light before. Nor did he feel he was displaying courage and faith.

He said, "I just knew I needed to work my way out." Drastic changes altered their lives, and it wasn't until years later that Carol realized the Lord had answered her prayers.

Carol said, "I remembered being taught in Dale Carnegie that when you have a problem, you should picture the worst possible outcome, then look at it squarely and say: If this is the worst that can happen, I can live with that. Dayle and I did that. We figured out the worst things that could happen. It was unreal how everything we listed plus about fifty times more came about! I've never seen such a brash of bad luck. It was like a nightmare that got worse and worse."

One of the most important lessons to be learned from Carol and Dayle's experience is that a man and woman, by the very inherent natures they possess, handle financial crisis differently. Not knowing and understanding this adds to the grief and heartache. Each sees the same situation from an entirely different angle. Men tend to view things objectively, and women analyze the loss emotionally. It becomes a time of great misunderstanding and desperate thinking, dangerous to the family unit. Just because a man reacts differently doesn't mean he doesn't care. On the other hand, he needs to be understanding when his wife seems to be emotionally falling apart.

Dayle saw their situation as just an interruption and something he would have to find a way to work through, and Carol saw it as the end of the world. She was pregnant with their fourth child and deeply depressed. Every day phone calls would come from creditors, and many times sheriff's deputies would come to her door to serve judgment papers when friends were there. They were six months behind on the house rent and low on food. The baby was born about six months before the final auction. This was the most devastating part for Carol. It was like a neon sign proclaiming their losses to the world. "You feel sick and desperate, and pride is your last possession," stated Carol.

Carol's bishop visited with her and asked if there was anything she needed, or if the children needed shoes. She was feeding the baby powdered milk from food storage, but said she was so proud that she refused help. Later, she said, "I wasn't smart enough then to be open with anybody and talk about it. I wouldn't allow anyone to help us. If it happened again, I would do it differently. I would accept temporary help from my bishop. I would take a food order. It was selfish of me to let my pride deprive my family of the things they needed."

The next few months Carol was so depressed that she was hardly functional. Although she never received medical help, she had all the symptoms of a nervous breakdown. She remembered, "I couldn't even do my dishes or decide what to wear. Unable to eat, I dropped a lot of weight." One weekend as she visited her parents' cabin, her mother noticed the children didn't have any socks without holes in them. She went to the store and bought socks. Carol mused, "It's funny how you compensate. Today my kids have drawers full of socks."

Although Dayle felt a terrible weight day and night, he never experienced depression nor did he lose faith in himself. The Teton Dam had just broken, and he got a job driving truck for HUD, hauling furniture to flood victims in Rexburg. It proved to be very therapeutic and a real blessing as every day he heard others' stories and was able to help someone else immediately after his own loss. At home, Carol suffered emotionally as Dayle, more stable and objective, was unable to understand and didn't realize until later the seriousness of her condition.

"Depression is really difficult to deal with if no one around you acknowledges it," noted Carol. "It's like having the flu, and someone thinks you should be up cleaning the house. I don't ever remember Dayle giving me a bad time or making it more difficult for me, but he wasn't able to support me in my trial. I felt like the heavens were closed. I was left all alone and isolated, but I never lost my testimony. I know now that the Lord is always there, but that He allowed Satan to come in and 'blast' me because He knew I would be okay. He wouldn't have allowed it if He hadn't known I could make it through."

For several months, Carol felt suicidal. Her mother recognized her condition and called her every morning with, "Hi, are you okay?" Carol remembered her being very calm and making sure all of the aspirins and other medications were out of Carol's house. "She and Dad didn't pay our bills, but they bought us food. We didn't need to be bailed out; we needed to learn some lessons." Every day the phone call came, and Carol would promise that she wouldn't commit suicide that day. It was just like AA, one day at a time for five or six months.

"It was such a dangerous time, because I was so weak," remembered Carol. Just as Satan tempted the Savior after He was weakened from fasting, he knew when I was most vulnerable and hit me with everything. I would cry myself to sleep every night. It was like a whole army of Satan's hosts were determined that they would get me. I was hit with every temptation possible. I thought I would never make it, but no matter how embarrassed I was with what I was feeling, I would talk to Mom each day about it and she would say, 'Carol, remember you are our Sunshine Girl, and you will make it.'

"It was very difficult to be around people, and I had to discipline myself to go to church. We went through a period of great contention. I blamed Dayle, and he felt that if I had helped him more it would never have happened. There is so much anger. Who can you blame but yourselves?"

She continued, "I remember riding down the road and seeing others who weren't really what you would call bright or talented, and yet they were taking care of themselves. I couldn't help but think, 'Are we so stupid that we can't even take care of ourselves?' I've found that is a common feeling. What's wrong with us? Are we really that stupid? It takes a long time to trust your own judgment again. Lots of people get in trouble financially, but most don't lose their homes. We lived in five different homes in two years just trying to exist. Few people experience total humiliation.

"We came so close to divorce that it is frightening. I was so down and desperate that I thought that if I could divorce Dayle, I could divorce the problem. And Dayle thought I was making a big deal out of it and blowing it out of proportion. As I look back on it now, I think that women many times do just that. We make it an even bigger obstacle. We need to be careful not to drag our mate down with us emotionally and find a way to pull ourselves up by the boot straps. Somehow we need to find a productive side, even if it's only going for a walk or doing a load of wash. We can discipline ourselves step-by-step to develop productivity instead of remaining overwhelmed and living in a state of emotional desperation."

Dayle, like most men, turned to work and tried to work it out. "All I could think of was, 'What are we going to do next,' or 'How are we going to get out of this mess?'" Men are more frequently able to compartmentalize their lives and categorize the problems and then organize steps to meet each segment. Carol feels that women need to realize that every little thing tends to flow over into every big thing in their lives. It would be very helpful for women to develop skills to help them put things in proper perspective, so they won't be overwhelmed.

Everything was gone, and it was frightening for the Holms to realize as the dust cleared that they owed a lot more than they were worth, and suddenly their occupation was gone. Where did one begin? Carol remembered thinking, "We were so old. Dayle was 37, and I was 33. I wondered how you could possibly start over at such an old age. We went to an attorney who counselled us to take out bankruptcy. At a time like that, you have tunnel vision and you can't think of any new options. You are so devastated it's hard to realize there are a lot of possibilities. A visit with our bishop helped us to see that we had options. We prayed to know if we should take out bankruptcy, and although we chose not to doesn't mean that others shouldn't. I've seen people that have chosen not to and then lived the rest of their lives in hell paying back old debt. It is a very personal decision. No one can judge anyone else. This has to be one that you decide with your mate, after you have received wise counsel.

"It was at this time that we decided that I should go back to work instead," said Carol. "I wholeheartedly agree with President Benson's counsel that a woman should be in the home, but I will also be the first to agree that we shouldn't go broke, either. We have to look at our own situations and have the courage to follow our own inspirations. We need to allow sisters the emotional freedom to make those kinds of choices. We can't put everybody in the same mold and put them on a guilt trip for following their own inspiration. That's what it's all about, inspiration. Other women I've talked to have found the answer is to stay home. Many times they face judgment for that decision, too. I received my answer powerfully, but it would be months before I had healed enough to go into the world."

Carol's parents had a home in Idaho Falls that became vacant, so Carol, Dayle, and their children moved there to not have to pay rent. In this new ward, members didn't see the normal bubbly Carol, but instead, a quiet, distant woman from whom no one expected anything. But good friends from the Blackfoot 8th Ward kept in contact and came to visit. True, good friends remain true. Great strength came from their encouraging words of "just know we love you."

A relative of Dayle's owned an excavating business in Rexburg, so Dayle worked the rest of the summer and through December levelling land destroyed by the flood. The next spring he worked tearing down demolished houses. He was then able to make a down payment on a used backhoe, his first piece of equipment, and start his own business again.

The family moved back to Blackfoot to a little house in the country that provided privacy and a place to heal. Carol commented, "You need to be left alone for time to heal. It takes too much energy to deal with your problems and handle everyone else. We needed some privacy as we tried to put our lives back together." After all the moving and trauma had ended, the learning period began, and the Holms could begin to see and understand their pitfalls.

During this period, Carol took one of her sons to a counselor for a kindergarten evaluation. The children had suffered from the tremendous upset in their lives. The counselor finished the consultation and announced the little boy was fine, but Carol was in real trouble and needed help. She had tried several times to call the Church Social Services for help, but she would either hang up when they answered or break the appointments she made. "I was too sick to forge ahead and take care of myself," she said. "It took someone from the outside to take my hand and help me. It is really important that we are aware of others and help them." The counselor offered to talk to Carol during his lunch hours, and she felt she could handle that. After three or four therapy sessions, Carol had learned to dig her emotions out from under the rug. After releasing buckets of tears and a broken heart, Carol was able to let go of a painful load.

Her baby was a year old, and Carol was beginning to heal. The little rental house had three feet of water in the basement, no washer or dryer, and little animals running around. Carol knew it was time to go to work. Realizing that it would be very tough, she decided on the insurance field, knowing she would get nowhere in helping her family recover by working for minimum wage. Her close friend and stake president, and also her bishop were concerned about her choice and the pressure she would face. But Carol knew that she had received answers to her prayers, and this was what she would do. She promised her bishop that she would always try to be home when the children got off the bus in the afternoon.

The family moved to another little home in town, and Carol's rigorous schedule began. She got up every morning at 5 a.m. to study and learn the business. Then she got the kids on the bus and was to the office by 8 a.m. Keeping her promise, she always tried to be home at 3:30 when the bus arrived. She would then fix supper and go back out to appointments at least three or four nights a week. Usually Carol would leave home at 6 or 7 p.m. and be out until 11. On Saturdays, she would do the laundry and cover the bases at home. This pace continued for at least two years before things started to take off.

About one year into the business Carol unexpectedly got pregnant. She had previously had the varicose veins in her legs stripped and had other health problems and wasn't supposed to have any more children. It was a very difficult time. The insurance company had never had a pregnant agent before and almost fired her. Carol's pride prevented her from contacting friends, and she had determined to do it all "cold call." So here she was, a pregnant stranger knocking on doors. She was understandably unable to do much until the baby was a year old.

Then a big year hit. Out of fifty agents, Carol was third in production. She received a lot of attention, and the company had big plans for her. In the meantime, the family had moved to the Thomas area and in the midst of Carol's tremendous professional success she was called as Relief Society president. It had only been four and one-half years since their great trauma, and inwardly Carol was still suffering. She was very active but still didn't want to open up and get closely attached in a ward.

The past few years had taken her from terrible experiences to tremendous success with everyone clamoring to know her secret. She could see that she would become top agent, and all of a sudden it was as though the Lord took hold of her ankles with Carol dragging by her fingernails pleading, "I'm not going to be Relief Society president! Not after all we've been through. Please, we have just gotten to where most of the debt is paid, and for the first time in years we can breathe and do something for ourselves. Please don't ask me to do this!"

Nevertheless, Carol accepted the call and diligently served for three years. Meanwhile, her production dropped, and her boss approached her about her record. She explained to him about Relief Society and why she couldn't do more, and he asked if the Church made her do it. She assured him that it didn't, and he shook his head and said, "You do all that, and you're telling me you have a choice." By this time, their oldest son was on a mission and their daughter in college. Every month was nip and tuck, but they made it.

As ward Relief Society president, Carol found that her experiences had developed within her a deep and inner concern for others and their problems. She knew where people were coming from. Being able to relate to nearly every trial, she grew to love and became close to the sisters in her ward.

Carol described as her greatest strength the ability to pray every night and day. She knew as did Nephi, that the Lord doesn't ask anything of us that He doesn't prepare a way.

"Being Relief Society president was the most challenging three years of my life. There were times when I didn't know if I could make it physically. Another great challenge I had to deal with was the criticism of those I loved in the gospel for working. I'm not a gentile mother because I work. It was a difficult load to carry paying off all the debt and having a small baby and an insurance business, and then go to church and feel others' judgment. We're not on opposite sides of the fence. We need to work together.

"Everyone has difficulties. I've found that when I sit down and tell others about all the stupid mistakes I've made, it makes them feel a little better. They think, 'If Carol has done it, maybe I'm not the only one.' I wouldn't trade the knowledge I've gained for anything. I've seen people who have never had failures look at others and think it's their own foolishness—the old "you made your own bed" attitude. So what, even if you have made your own bed. It is just like a child when he learns to walk. He falls down and then gets up and falls down again. Sometimes we don't seem to have the patience to allow people to come through the process. We want them to be running when they ought to be creeping and crawling and falling down. That's part of life. If you're going to reach out and do something that's over your head, you are going to fall and get up and fall again. But wouldn't you rather have someone do that than just lie in bed? Successful people know of what I speak because most of them have been there."

Dayle said, "We were just a couple of ambitious kids, with more ambition than smarts. The attitude we developed from Dale Carnegie course may have been what got us into trouble, but it is also what got us out. And the Lord blessed us and helped us. Your life changes the more diligently you serve and the more honestly you pay tithing. We were paying tithing when we went broke, but perhaps on a lesser principle, because we had to borrow to pay. Each year we improved in the way we paid our tithing, and as we did, we became more successful."

Carol and Dayle had the courage to try, and through their example, many others have been inspired not to give up. They continue to work hard supporting the community and the church. Carol is now serving in the stake Relief Society presidency, and Dayle is ward clerk.

They are frequently complimented on their

tremendous talent and ability. But how would one survive such an experience without developing a tremendous talent to survive and cope? They both agree that they would hate to go through it again. However, they would trade nothing for what they have learned. They offer this advice to others:

1. Don't feel embarrassed or that you have to hide. Carol remembered feeling so dishonest when creditors came for money, and she couldn't pay them. You may have made critical mistakes, but you are not unworthy or dishonest.

2. Carol recalled that when she first went to work she had such a strong desire to prove that she wasn't stupid. "Now I realize that was quite foolish. Nobody is even caring. It doesn't make any difference to those guys. You think people are sitting around wondering about you. They're not. They're worrying about themselves. We worried far too much about what everyone else was thinking."

3. Get sufficient education in the field you want to pursue. Knowledge and education are power and protection.

4. Realize that any time you go into business for yourself there are risks. There are also risks involved with working for someone else. You could lose your job. Many of the same symptoms that Carol experienced are common to women whose husbands

have been unemployed for long periods of time. No one in this society is immune to problems.

5. When problems arise, work diligently to provide more than just survival for your family. They need emotional security. You may have lost all of your self-esteem, but somehow find a way to hold it together for them. Losing the security of the family unit has long-lasting effects on children.

6. Be willing to share yourself with others. Said Carol, "Too often we don't know many things about others until they are gone. We tend to be so private that we don't share what we've been through. People need to be more open about their true selves, so we can get clear pictures. All we usually see is the 'gloss and the glitz stuff.' How can we see a true vision of life and how people got to where they are now, if all we see is the gloss? I guess that's why I'm so open. If I'm willing to admit some of the mistakes I've made, then perhaps you can admit some of yours, and we can get on with life.

"The most important thing I've learned," Carol shared, "is I have what it takes to make it through any problem. I think I am capable of pulling through any trial that could come to me. That gives me a lot of self-esteem. As I look to the last days and contemplate all the things that could happen to us, I have a deep and abiding assurance that I can do it. I'm not saying that I will, but that I *can*. What a fantastic concept! With the Lord's help, I'm capable and so are you."

CHAPTER TEN

Miracle of Renewal

Dorothy

"Be still and know that I am God."

The walk down the corridor of the LDS hospital to the radiation department seemed interminable. Arrows directing the way lead from carpeted floors to shiny tile. As our footsteps continued the sound became louder and louder and could only be offset by the pounding of my heart.

This was not the way I had planned to spend the Christmas holidays. I loved Christmas. I looked forward to it from January to the following Christmas and by September I was playing the beloved carols. I often wondered what the UPS delivery man thought when he came Halloween day and was met with the strains of *Joy to the World.* I could see that today would be anything but joy in my world.

As I approached the waiting room, I could see chairs filled with people of all ages, with one thing in common—looking sad in spite of the cheerful nurses and technicians. The expressionless faces gazed into nowhere with empty eyes. "These people are sick," I told myself. "I can't be one of them!"

My turn finally came. Forms had to be filled out. Height and weight were checked and then I was shown a row of lockers and was instructed to strip to the waist and put on a robe and return to the waiting room. This became my routine for the next six weeks.

As I looked around at all of the invisibly labeled cancer victims sitting in the waiting room, I again asked myself what I was doing here. There had to be a mistake. Mistakes are made all the time. Across from me sat the handsome healthy-looking football player, the young mother of two beautiful children, the pretty model, and the man with a stocking cap on his head which he never removed. Next to him sat his wife whose fingers moved constantly turning out varied knitted items to keep herself occupied so she would not have to think. And then there was the older couple, she with beautiful white hair and he with eyes only for her. He appeared very ill.

I was soon ushered in to see the doctors. Both very considerate women who checked and rechecked me and sent me to a radiation therapist who directed me to disrobe and lay on the X-ray table. There I immediately realized why it had been so important for me to do the "walk up the wall" exercises to regain the use of my arm again after the cancer surgery six weeks before. I had to lie flat on my back, with my left arm straight up and then brought back down to touch my shoulder. I was instructed to turn my head to the right with my chin over my right shoulder. It was imperative that I lie perfectly still. For two hours X-rays were taken and the marking process was monitored by the doctors on a screen. Every precaution was taken for the procedure to be just right. The breast had to be marked around the surgical incision so the technicians giving the radiation treatments would make no mistakes.

Being positive about life had never been a problem for me. If a situation couldn't be changed or resolved, you simply went on and did the best you could. Why was this so different? I couldn't do anything about my situation now. My husband, Lorin, my children and friends were doing everything they could to make my situation easier, but I just couldn't be positive about life right now. It was out of control. I moved like a robot, following instructions and feeling as if I was slipping into lonely oblivion.

As I walked out of the office that day, I determined I would not return! A smothering, black feeling engulfed me and life held little meaning. "What is wrong with you, there are people who have life so much harder than you," I reprimanded. I forced myself to think of others I had seen suffer so terribly and I tried to tell myself that if I were in their shoes then I would have something to complain about. But the chastisement was to no avail. I could only deal with one thing at a time and right now there just wasn't room to be concerned for others.

The next morning, the final decision was in. I knew I had to stay and follow doctors' instructions. Lorin helped me move into the apartment and did everything he could to help me be comfortable before he had to leave. As we knelt in prayer I could feel his deep concern for me. I had always tried to be cheerful, but this time I felt as if I had nothing left. I could not see any light at the end of the tunnel in which I felt encased. What was it I had heard my mother say so often? "Do not curse the darkness. Light one candle." If she were here with me now she would probably tell me how important it was to light the way for another. But for now, all I could see was myself.

As I finished unpacking, I noticed a wrapped gift a friend had brought over the night before, with the caution, "It is not to be opened now." As I picked it up I saw the writing on top, "Do not open until you can stand it no longer." I lingered with it in my hands. Who could say what lay ahead. I placed it in the bottom drawer of the dresser. "How can it get any worse than it is now?" I wondered.

In the waiting room before my first treatment, I thumbed through a magazine and blankly stared at the pages. "How could this be happening to me? What had happened to my life?"

Three months ago I was so happy. Everything was great. I had been to visit my children and on my return home, I had such an uneasy feeling that something was wrong. Of course everything was all right so it was easy to dismiss such thoughts. Had it only been three months? For a few moments my mind raced wildly back to the first week in September as the plane circled the Salt Lake City area. Anxiously I peered through the small window at the topography below. The land was so colorful, and the changing of the season was evident. The scenery was familiar and it meant I was almost home. Home! Even though it was still a three-hour drive to our home in Pingree, I would be with Lorin and that was the most important thing. He was standing where I could see him as I walked down the concourse. That was the way it had been for 39 years. Lorin was always there. I was so happy to see him, but even in my happiness, the feeling of foreboding returned. Had that been a warning of some kind? If so, I was just too happy to acknowledge it.

This was one of the many such trips when Lorin had met me in Salt Lake after a visit to the children. The three older children were married and between them they had given Lorin and me nine wonderful grandchildren. In five months the youngest grandson would be home from his mission in Denmark. I had every day planned right up to his arrival, at least I thought as much then.

How I loved serving as stake Relief Society president in the Blackfoot West Stake. There was much to do to prepare for the upcoming Relief Society auxiliary training meeting. I loved the women in my stake. They truly loved the Lord. It was while I was preparing for presidency meeting that I found the lump. How quickly life can change.

I was brought back to reality with a start as I heard, "Mrs. Casper, we are ready for you now."

I was staying at a home provided for radiation patients at a nominal fee. As I walked back after the treatment I was so lonesome, and felt such an indescribable emptiness. I climbed the stairs to the second floor and when I reached my room, I dropped to my knees with a plea. "Please, Father, tell me what I should do. Help me to feel something inside besides sadness. Please help me to do more than just exist, not simply bide my time, and help me to forget myself."

I picked up a little notebook I had beside my bed and listed things I could do. I was behind in my journal; I needed to write letters; and I would go to the temple as long as I could handle it physically. I would look for the miracles, and before I went to bed at night I would list my blessings. I knew the Lord did not zap me with cancer, but I had it and He expected me to learn from the experience. The tears burned the back of my eyelids but I refused to let them surface. Somehow maybe I can light the way for another. I would begin by pretending life was good and I would not permit anyone to know otherwise.

The first week was almost over. My treatments had been scheduled at 8:00 a.m. and I would leave to go over to the hospital as soon as I talked to my son. He called every morning at 7:45. I almost wondered if my husband and children got together and planned their calls. It seemed they would each contact me just when

I needed it most.

In the walk to the hospital, the winter air was cold and brisk and the snowflakes whirled in the wind. Everyone seemed to draw their coats a little closer to keep away the chill. No one looked up, but somehow I had to try to keep the goal I had made the night before. "Good morning," I said. A warm feeling entered my heart and I realized I meant it. As I entered the radiation department something had changed. The remodeling was still in full force, but there was a look and feel of Christmas in the air. Decorations were plentiful and a tree stood tall in the corner and was being decorated by the nurses and technicians. I noticed a nurse's aid roll a patient in on her bed. I had seen her before, but she always had a gentleman with her who I assumed was her husband. This time she was alone. The aid said, "I'll leave you right here and someone will come and get you when they are ready to give you your treatment. I will come for you when you are through. The patient did not respond. I was prompted to speak as I passed by her to get dressed, but I did not speak. After my treatment was complete, I noticed she was still there. I had another chance.

"Good morning," I said. "How are you feeling today?" Silence prevailed as I waited for her to answer. "Are you from around Salt Lake?" "Do you really want to know?" the lady answered with guarded reservation. "Yes, I do," I replied. "I really do. I have seen you here and wanted to speak to you. I can see you are a very interesting person." A slight smile crossed her face as she replied, "I used to be, but I have been here so long

now that . . . ." Her voice trailed off as she shook her
head sadly. Then she added, "I'm from Southern Utah
and I have 22 grandchildren, and I really miss them. I
suppose they have forgotten me by now." My eyes
brimmed with tears. I hoped she wouldn't notice.
"Why don't I get a pen and paper and you can tell me
what to write and we will make sure they don't forget
you," I volunteered. A look of sincere gratitude covered
her face. Such a small gesture from me, and yet so
important to her. I must never forget how little effort is
required to make another happy. "Father, thank you,"
my heart cried. "I'm on the right track." The sweet
words of love and encouragement from a grandmother
to her children brought to mind the words of a little
poem.

> Just around the corner of my life
> Sadness awaits.
> I cry, "No, not now."
> Another greater than I
> In silence whispers, "I'm here.
> Just one more step, my child.
> Don't try to do more.
> It seems long,
> But it's only a while.
> First the rain,
> Then the sun
> And the rainbow comes with a smile."[1]

---

[1] Dorothy Casper, *I'm Here*, 1989.

I was finally able to emerge from the darkness into the light and could feel the presence of the Father whisper, "I'm here." Perhaps I was learning. At least for a time I could forget myself. As I walked out into the winter snowstorm, I was sure I could see a rainbow through the flakes of snow.

Every morning before I went to the hospital, I prayed the Lord would guide me to the things I should do and the right words to say to those I came in contact with. I was at the hospital about a half-hour and the actual treatment took about five minutes, so there was 25 minutes I could use to help someone. I prayed, too, that I would accept my circumstances gracefully and not look on them at anytime as futile. I read somewhere that "Life affords no greater pleasure than that of surmounting difficulties." Too often we desire the pleasure, without the difficulty. The question I had asked myself so many times when I first came to Salt Lake returned again. I asked, "Why did this happen to me?" Suddenly I realized, "Why not? I am no different than anyone else." The motto I had lived by for a long time again appeared in my mind. Me + God = Enough. I must not forget it again.

Later in the week the little white-haired lady was all alone when I reached the hospital. Her husband had already gone in for his treatment. I sat down beside her and asked how he was doing. Each week the patients were given a checkup to see how the radiation treatments were progressing. His reports had not been favorable. When he approached us, we visited for a few moments. When he expressed how discouraged he was, his wife patted him on the knee and said, "Honey, this is not the end. It is just another of life's interruptions. Little did I realize the impact those words would have on my life for a long time to come.

The treatments were becoming more difficult since the cancer was located underneath the sternum. The heart and lungs were becoming damaged in spite of the doctor's best efforts. On my way back to the "home" following the treatments, I ran into difficulty. The walk that should have taken only a few minutes turned into a half-hour. I could not breathe very well and my heart rate was so fast I had to stop and rest several times on my walk up the hill. When I reached my room I collapsed on the bed and could no longer hold back the tears. I lay there pleading with the Lord to please give me the strength to go on. I did not know if this would be the worst, but right then I couldn't handle any more. With shaking hands, I opened the drawer in the dresser to get some medicine and there was the little gift and the note which said, "Open me when you can stand it no longer."

I ripped the paper open. Inside was a homely little cock-eyed reindeer. Antlers awry and tied to his neck was a small card which read, "When things get to be too much, you can stomp me, kick me, hit me or throw me against the wall, but I will still be your friend. I was startled as I looked at the furry ball. I began to laugh and cry at the same time. When I knelt in prayer that night after counting the miracles of the day and the miracle of my little friend, another beautiful miracle occurred as I felt the words, "Lo, I am with you always."

"When you have done it unto the least of these you have done it unto me" was a teaching I had used many times in encouraging women in the wards with visiting teaching, etc.

Now as so many of his children served me I felt his presence.

The holidays were such a busy time and yet they found time for me. It seemed the more I tried to reach out to others in treatment, the more I received.

Our plans to leave on December 15 and attend our son's graduation from Emery University and to visit the other children for the holidays were not to be. Lorin spent it in Salt Lake with me.

Many changes had taken place in our lives. I was released from my position as Relief Society president. I would miss the strength and the closeness that we had and the spiritual times we shared.

Christmas came—though not as planned. For the first time in 39 years, Lorin and I were alone on Christmas Eve. We would spend Christmas Day with our son and his family, but tonight it would be just the two of us. As we sat in front of the little tree, Lorin read the Christmas story from the scriptures, in keeping with the tradition we always cherished. As we knelt together in prayer, my heart swelled with joy as I thought of all the kindnesses which had been extended to us and made life much easier. Gratefully I recalled the memories of the friend who was ill herself but still always had time to check on me. The gentle soul who said, "I didn't bring you food for the body, but food for

the soul," and handed me several video tapes. The
neighbor who ran in every morning to see if there were
errands to run, or to change my bandage; and the
children who brought the little decorated Christmas
tree and tears filled my eyes. Never would I forget all
the food and other kindnesses provided by the women
in my ward. The cards and letters of encouragement.
The flowers and other gifts which all said, "We care!"
Each of our children and grandchildren adding
support in every way.

Wasn't this the true meaning of Christmas?
Surely I had been the recipient of Christ-like love and
giving.

Early Christmas morning Lorin jumped out of
bed and hurried into the living room to turn the lights
on on our little tree. The two of us sat on the floor
around it and opened our gifts. The lights on the tree
were not half as bright as the light that glowed in my
heart. I would treasure this moment always. It was a
beautiful experience to be with my eternal mate and
companion, just the two of us in the quiet peace of
Christmas morning. What a blessed gift to know of the
Babe born in Bethlehem. How grateful I was for
Heavenly Father who loved me so much that He sent
His Son to die for me, and a Son who loved me so much
He gave His life for me. Perhaps for the first time I
experienced the true miracle of Christmas.

January 15, 1988 was a red-letter day; the last
day of treatment. I could go home. The word had never
sounded so good. I had made it. It was over. Life could
return to its normal everyday, mundane tasks which

now would never again be taken for granted. Every flower, every tree, every blade of grass would be appreciated by me. Never again would I take life for granted. I could hardly wait for the snow to leave and for spring to come, so I could be outside again, to work in the flowers. They had always been very therapeutic to frazzled nerves.

One last checkup before leaving for home. The doctors gave me a thorough examination. Everything was explained and appointments for follow-ups were made. Just before I was to get dressed, I needed to ask the most critical question.

"Am I cured, or do I still have cancer?"

"Yes," she replied, "you are cured right now, but don't ask me in five minutes."

That was not the answer I had hoped for. I wanted to leave the Center knowing that the last six weeks had not been in vain, and that my life would finally return to normal. I wanted a guarantee there would be no more of life's interruptions.

"Are you saying I could have cancer again anytime?" I questioned further.

She folded her arms, leaned against the file cabinet, and stared at the floor for a moment as if searching for just the right words.

"Dorothy," she asked, "what difference does it make?"

For a moment I was almost angry. To me it makes a lot of difference. And then I slowly realized what she was trying to say.

"Go home, continue to love life, to use what you

have learned and go forward." Too much is lost when you dwell on what might be.

What difference did it make? She was right. Be it cancer, old age, or a fatal walk across the street, life for each of us is terminal. We must live every minute to its fullest, for each one spent will never return. Whether it be sorrow and heartache, or uncertainty, the more we dwell on it the less we have. We must not allow those things to diminish from the good things in life. Grief and adversity must be put in their proper places. We need to deal with them when they can do some good when the pain is actually there, not just anticipated.

By constantly dwelling on our problems, we spoil the beauty of the moment.

The thirty treatments were marked off on the calendar and I could not understand why my body would not cooperate with me. I had it planned that life would be normal again, but not so. Some people who have radiation suffer ill effects, one being pneumonitis. Such was my new interruption. It manifested itself as a severe case of pneumonia. I struggled with extreme tiredness, severe coughing, chills and high fever.

Unlike other respiratory diseases, it does not respond to antibiotics. For several weeks there was no relief and the next three months were to become the most difficult time of my life.

Each day became more difficult and I became weaker. It now required more effort to walk across the floor than my usual four-mile daily walk. Air was my most precious commodity. The nights were filled with fear that life-giving air would be cut off completely. The

words of the Psalmist often came to mind and I took
Him at His word.

"And call upon me in the day of troubles; and I
will deliver thee."

Endless nights turned to agonizing days. Days
and nights seemed to run together.

I now began to understand that even when life
brings an overwhelming interruption, we still have to
face daily sorrows and trials. A new and very personal
heartache entered my life and brought me emotional
and spiritual pain as intense as my physical suffering.
I groped for answers but couldn't resolve my inner
feelings. Again I chastised myself and determined to
try harder, but no peace came.

I gathered new strength and decided that each
day I would try to walk around to at least one of the
flower beds to see if any of the perennials had made it
through the long hard winter. After several days of
close inspection, I realized I would just have to plant
again. "When will this end?" I bitterly thought as I
counted the ironies of the past few months. "They will
never make it and neither will I." It was as though our
lives were symbolically linked desperately needing
renewal and the strength to survive available only from
above.

I answered the phone early one morning to a
voice which asked,"Sister Dorothy Casper?"

"Yes," I replied.

"This is Vaughn Featherstone. You have a very
good friend who loves you and is concerned about you."

He went on to explain how he knew of my illness

and then asked me how I was feeling. As he continued to talk to me, I began to hear the answers I had been struggling with and praying about. For one of the Lord's busiest servants to take time for me was so gratifying and very humbling. Our conversation brought the relief I so desperately needed. Even though physically, there remained a mountain to climb, I had now received inspiration to help me understand some of the injustices of life.

The next morning dawned a beautiful spring day. I was determined that I would walk all around the lawn and stop at each flower bed. If there was no sign of life, I would have to make plans to replant, so there would be beautiful flowers to enjoy. As I stopped to rest at the edge of the first bed, I could hardly believe my eyes. There were little green shoots everywhere, each reaching upward to the light and straining for the warmth of the sun. Another of God's miracles— the miracle of life.

Just like the perennials, I too had come through the long hard winter. I had reached for the warmth and strained for the light. Light that only God could give. As He gently guided and I often resisted, His love continued. Everywhere I looked and everything I did was indeed a gift from God. I had never truly noticed all the beauties of His creations until now, but never again would I take them for granted. I would remember each kindness and I would return it to another.

Yes, each day brings its own priceless miracle— the renewal of life and a promise of tomorrow.